**JOURNAL FOR THE STUDY OF THE OLD TESTAMENT
SUPPLEMENT SERIES**
164

Editors
David J.A. Clines
Philip R. Davies

Executive Editor
John Jarick

Editorial Board
Richard J. Coggins, Alan Cooper, Tamara C. Eskenazi,
J. Cheryl Exum, Robert P. Gordon, Norman K. Gottwald,
Andrew D.H. Mayes, Carol Meyers, Patrick D. Miller

JSOT Press
Sheffield

House of God or House of David

The Rhetoric of 2 Samuel 7

Lyle Eslinger

Journal for the Study of the Old Testament
Supplement Series 164

Copyright © 1994 Sheffield Academic Press

Published by JSOT Press
JSOT Press is an imprint of
Sheffield Academic Press Ltd
343 Fulwood Road
Sheffield S10 3BP
England

Typeset by Sheffield Academic Press
and
Printed on acid-free paper in Great Britain
by Bookcraft Ltd
Midsomer Norton, Bath

British Library Cataloguing in Publication Data

A catalogue record for this book is available
from the British Library

ISBN 1-85075-481-0

for Alan Cooper
in gratitude

Contents

Figures

PREFACE

This book is a contination of work begun in *Into the Hands of the Living God* (Sheffield: JSOT, 1989), a study devoted to the so-called "key speeches" in the Dtr narratives. Having completed those studies, I became increasingly convinced by Dennis McCarthy's argument ("II Samuel 7 and the Structure of the Deuteronomic History," *JBL* 84 (1965), 131–8) that 2 Samuel 7 deserved a reckoning among the key rhetorical passages in the narrative. In the beginning I imagined that the work would involve nothing more than a careful analysis of what had come to be known as "Nathan's oracle," the foundational text for the so-called "Davidic covenant." But the passage quickly staked its own rhetorical claims on what it was "about." I ceased work on "Nathan's oracle," of which the chapter contains but a fragment, and became involved with the rhetorical tug-of-war between Yahweh and David, which occupies the bulk of the chapter's 29 verses.

Based on my reading of the interaction between Yahweh and Solomon in 1 Kgs 1–11 I had hoped to find some clue about Yahweh's reasons for dishonouring his "eternal covenant" with David when it came to David's son, Solomon (*Hands of God*, pp. 137–8, 147). Reading on the basis of the conventional reading of 2 Samuel 7, the very parchment of the "Davidic covenant," I supposed that God, being God, simply reneged on the agreement for his own unknowable godly purpose. For me, the conditionalization of the "unconditional" covenant raised ethical questions and also suspicions that the narrative contained its own misgivings about the divine performance in history (*Hands of God*, pp. 178–79). But now, having made my own investigation of the procedings in 2 Samuel 7, I believe that what God does with Solomon is no more than to make explicit what is hidden, only somewhat, in the promises to David. There is no retroactive conditionalization because the Sinaitic conditions are embedded in the very heart of the so-called Davidic covenant. More accurately, the Davidic covenant as such, never existed except in the minds of those taken in by Yahweh's seductive rhetoric in 2 Samuel 7.

It remains for me to thank those who have helped me improve the manuscript. Thanks, to Anthony Campbell, for his contribution and sharp eyes for typographical errors in the long methodological excursus; to my colleague, Rob Cousland, for suggested improvements to the same; to J. Webb Mealy, Production Editor for *JSOT*; to the editors, for accepting the book; and especially to my student David Bergen, for proofing the entire manuscript.

The work is dedicated to my teacher, Alan Cooper. While working with Sheffield on the publication of my dissertation (*Kingship of God in Crisis* [Sheffield, 1985]), a communications foul up prevented me from expressing my gratitude for his supervision of the thesis. I hope that this third piece is neither too far from the standard that Alan established for my first work on the Deuteronomistic history nor too late to constitute a sincere expression of gratitude for his influence. No student could ask for a better model of a love of learning and scholarship.

ABBREVIATIONS

AJBI	*Annual of the Japanese Biblical Institute*
Bib	*Biblica*
BZAW	Beihefte zur *ZAW*
CBQ	*Catholic Biblical Quarterly*
HUCA	*Hebrew Union College Annual*
JAOS	*Journal of the American Oriental Society*
JBL	*Journal of Biblical Literature*
JSOT	*Journal for the Study of the Old Testament*
JSOTSup	*Journal for the Study of the Old Testament*, Supplement Series
RHPR	*Revue d'histoire et de philosophie religieuses*
ST	*Studia theologica*
TDOT	G.J. Botterweck and H. Ringgren (ed.), *Theological Dictionary of the Old Testament*
VT	*Vetus Testamentum*
ZAW	*Zeitschrift für die alttestamentliche Wissenschaft*

Chapter 1

RHETORIC AND PERSUASION IN 2 SAMUEL 7

2 Samuel 7, with its "Davidic covenant," is a focal point for many important issues in the modern study of the Bible, but most specifically for research on the topic of covenant.[1] The text has been combed for deuteronomistic ideology, for its influence on Israelite covenantal theology, and perhaps also for elemental precursors to Jewish and Christian messianism. 2 Samuel 7 is crucial for covenantal studies since it has seemed, in conjunction with a handful of other biblical texts, to suggest a second, non-Sinaitic model for the covenant concept. The relationship between what God says to David in 2 Samuel 7 and the Sinai covenant has dominated discussion of this passage and scholarship has become polarized by it. In an article reviewing the state of the question ("The Davidic Covenant and Its Modern Interpreters"), Jon Levenson suggested that two approaches, "integrationist" or "segregationist," have dominated research (Levenson 1979:207). Integrationists try to resolve the apparent conflict between the two, either by subsuming one within the other (usually the Davidic within the Sinaitic), by suggesting a historical succession from Sinaitic to Davidic (e.g., Gileadi 1988), or by ranging the two as somewhat complementary descriptions of a complex covenantal relationship between God and Israel (e.g., Waltke 1988).[2] Segregationists have seen mostly irresolvable differences between Sinaitic and Davidic covenants (e.g., Bright 1976) and so try to comprehend the two statements within a framework of historical development or social diversity in ancient Israel.[3]

---

1. "2 Sam 7 is, without doubt, the theological highlight of the Books of Samuel (so Stolz, 220) if not of the Deuteronomistic History as a whole" (A.A. Anderson 1989:112; for a recent bibliography of 2 Sam 7 scholarship see pp. 109–10 in Anderson or A.F. Campbell (1986:72 n. 19).

2. William Dumbrell (1988) adds a new wrinkle to the integrationists' proposal by pointing out the strong *unconditional* elements in the Sinaitic covenant.

3. Levenson himself proposes a mediating solution in which there are both "Sinaitic" (conditional) and "Davidic" (unconditional) aspects to the Davidic covenant because the royal Zionist traditions have absorbed Sinai traditions (1985:188–206). Levenson's mediating view is anticipated by A.H.J. Gunneweg (1960:339–40).

At least one of the reasons for continuing disagreement about the Davidic covenant is the text of 2 Samuel 7 itself, or rather the dialogue in the text. 2 Samuel 7 presents the reader with three voices (four if the reticent narratorial voice be included), each expressing self-contradictory views. First David will build a temple (v. 2) and then he will not (vv. 18, 27). Nathan supports the project (v. 3) and then demurs (vv. 5, 17). Most troubling, for anyone seeking a stable ideological view on the issues of temple and covenant, Yahweh refuses but then allows a temple, refusing for "Sinaitic" reasons (vv. 6–7) but then weakening with "Davidic" ones (vv. 11–13). Depending on which voice a reader favours, one will arrive at a different view of the affair. Worse yet, the voices shift so that a fixation on what Yahweh says first (vv. 6–7) will see an Sinaitic ideology in the chapter, while a reader who attends God's concluding words (e.g. vv. 11–13) is more than likely to come away believing in a "Davidic" covenant. Given the apparent self-contradictions, three characters, each controverting himself, making for six variations, it is not difficult to understand that there should be disagreement about 2 Samuel 7.

The feature problems that critical readers have discovered in 2 Samuel 7 can be systematized under the symbolic categories of the chapter's past, present, and future relations in the Deuteronomistic narrative. The past is problematic because we see a conflict between the so-called unconditional Davidic and the conditional Sinaitic covenants.[1] The Sinaitic agreement can be terminated, an end catalyzed by Israel's defection; the Davidic, however, is "eternal" (2 Sam 7.13) and sin should not be just cause for termination. The context for such analysis has been the history of Israelite religion as expressed in and known from the biblical text. Remarkably, in this debate the existing context of these statements in 2 Samuel 7, and most important within Yahweh's speech to David, has not played a prominent role. Certainly the debate has been about details in the text, which are individually abundantly known and presented, but these details have not been studied so carefully in context as they might.

The present, the synchronic horizon of 2 Samuel 7, is problematic because the chapter seems to include literary discontinuities that might be resolved by literary analysis in a historical frame. Literary-critical

---

1. For a recent reiteration of the distinction see Jeremiah Unterman's article, "Covenant" (1985:191).

analysis of 2 Samuel 7 concerns itself mostly with the fit between varying statements within the chapter. There are two large speeches (three in all when David's provocative false start [v. 2] is included): the first from God to David (vv. 5–16; 12 verses); the second, David's response to God (vv. 18–29; 12 verses). Most perceived disjunctions lie within God's speech, but there are discontinuities between the speeches of God and David too. David's response is rarely suspect in and of itself. Its dogged grip on matters of dynasty is taken as comparative testimony both to the dissipate state of the divine speech and the author/editor's focal point. God's speech includes two different, seemingly unrelated topics: a rejection of David's desire to house the ark in a temple (vv. 5b–7) and a promise of Davidic dynasty (vv. 8–16). Explicit connection between the two topics does not surface until v. 13a, when God tells David that a promised descendent (v. 12) will be the one to build the afore-rejected temple (vv. 5b–7). P.K. McCarter's reading of v. 13a is representative: "This half-verse, then, is the linchpin of the passage. When it is removed, the oracle falls apart: there is no other reference in vv. 11b–16 to a temple, and there is no reference in vv. 5b–7 to David's offspring" (McCarter 1984:222; cf. M. Tsevat 1980:115). The question then becomes which topic was added to the other and the weight of argument falls on the plausibility of a redactional analysis and on the degree to which it interlocks with our understanding of other pieces in the Dtr redactional puzzle.[1]

And so, the future. The third concern about 2 Samuel 7 is the conflict between the "unconditional" promise of unending dynasty to David and the sorry end to the dynasty in 2 Kings, some 400 years later. Here the issue is much the same as the conflict with the past, though now the conflict is with the fruits born of conditionality. The story already begins to move towards exile with God's threats against David's immediate successor (1 Kgs 9.6–9) and perhaps even with David himself (2 Sam 12.10). Here we face a primary conflict within the narrative (R. Nelson 1981:27–28, 99–118). How to reconcile God's words to David—"I will establish the throne of his kingdom forever"—with the end of the story, Jehoiachin's release from the Babylonian

---

1. McCarter provides good comparative reviews of the various redactional analyses (1984:222–23).

prison (2 Kgs 25.27–30)?[1] The most common solution now is to suppose that the author who wrote the unconditional promises of 2 Samuel 7 did not envision the catastrophic portrait with which the book of 2 Kings now concludes (e.g., Cross 1973:287–89).

RHETORICAL ANALYSIS OF 2 SAMUEL 7

How to solve such problems? Perhaps we may cut a new path into 2 Samuel 7. This route is appropriate to the dialogic content of 2 Samuel 7 and requires only two exegetical tools: close reading, barely a method, and rhetorical analysis. 2 Samuel 7 has been read a lot, but not that "closely."[2] Of course, people have spent a lot of time studying the chapter and every detail has been remarked many times. Still, a "close reading" of the chapter might add a new perspective on the three horizons of "Davidic covenant" research by burying our glance in the microscopic details of the text, especially in their place in the logic of character rhetoric in this passage. Jan Fokkelman's commentary shows just how much of the text's detail is open to new insights from close reading.[3] As for rhetorical analysis, formal analyses of the type launched by James Muilenburg in his call for "rhetorical criticism" (1969), are only part of the task.[4]

In his manual for N.T. rhetorical criticism, George Kennedy outlines four steps in a rhetorical analysis: defining the rhetorical unit, defining the situation that elicited the piece, deciding on the "species" of rhetoric, and analyzing its structure and rhetorical devices (1984:33–38; cf. Corbett 1990:22–27). Muilenburg's discussion of the rhetorical method begins by defining the unit, but then skips to

---

1. The concluding scene of 2 Kings seems, to many, anything but a hopeful portrait, especially in the light of 2 Sam 7 (F.M. Cross, 1973:277). Dissenters, however, do exist: see Nelson (1981:149 n. 8) for a review of the opposing reading.

2. Jan Fokkelman's work (1990) is an obvious exception. Often, his commentary is the only source of comment on the text's detail.

3. Fokkelman himself calls for and then supplies a fresh reading of the text to get round the "framework rampant with prejudice" that he says historical-critical scholarship has constructed around this text (1990:207). I do not propose to duplicate or supplant Fokkelman's painstaking stylistic analysis, but to build a rhetorical analysis on the foundation laid by Fokkelman.

4. Cf. Dale Patrick, Alan Scult, (1990:12).

structural/stylistic analysis (1969:8–17).[1] Though Kennedy's "species" definition might be subsumed in an analysis of rhetorical or structural specifics, Muilenburg's omission of rhetorical context was a mistake that stunted the study of Hebrew rhetoric and the development of Old Testament rhetorical criticism. Structural and stylistic analyses, which have often seemed to degenerate into vapid appreciations of biblical literary genius and "unity," need the complement of careful attention to the argumentative aspects of biblical rhetoric taken in the context of the rhetorical situation as we may know it. Structural arrangement and rhetorical devices are only tools used by a speaker (or writer) to make an argument. Our primary concern for the rhetoric that we find within the narrative should be the strategies and rhetorical moves by which characters seek to persuade or bend each other to their own purpose.[2] The study of Old Testament rhetoric needs to follow the lead of recent studies of rhetorical forms in the N.T. (e.g., Betz 1979; Wuellner 1987). Burton Mack summarizes the goals of the "new rhetoric":

> By linking the persuasive power of a speech not only to its logic of argumentation, but to the manner in which it addresses the social and cultural history of its audience and speaker, Perelman and Olbrechts-Tyteca demonstrated the rhetorical coefficient that belongs to every human exchange involving speech, including common conversation and the daily discourse of a working society. This takes rhetoric out of the sphere of mere ornamentation, embellished literary style, and the extravagances of public oratory, and places it at the center of a social theory of language. On this model, rhetorical performance belongs to human discourse just as surely as stance and style belong to any presentation of ourselves at moments of personal encounter. Rhetoric is to a society and its discourse what grammar is to a culture and its language. Rhetoric refers to the rules of the language games agreed upon as acceptable within a given society. The rules of a rhetoric can be identified and studied, just as the rules of a grammar. Interest in such a rhetoric is grounded in the observation that the way we talk to each other is very serious business (1990:16).

---

1. Cf. M. Kessler (1974; 1980); I.M. Kikawada (1977). Wilhelm Wuellner (1987:451) criticizes the school of Muilenburg for reducing rhetorical analysis to an atrophying branch of literary stylistics at the expense of a rhetorical criticism centrally concerned with rhetoric as read and valued in its social context.

2. Cf. Kennedy (1984:3), "Rhetoric is that quality in discourse by which a speaker or writer seeks to accomplish his purposes."

Of course there is nothing in 2 Samuel 7 to compare to the rhetorical peregrinations of someone like the apostle Paul. Neither am I suggesting that we should look for fully developed classical rhetorical forms in the speech of David or Yahweh, though a better grasp of Hebrew rhetoric in its A.N.E. context may some day bring us to that turn. Rather, we find non-conventional argumentation (at least we do not have the needed comparative documentation to detect use of formal conventions) that reveals strategy and motivation. Every word, every turn of phrase or topic can reveal to us what it is that Yahweh and David are trying to accomplish in their verbal fencing. Not to say, either, that rhetorical strategy in the narratives of the Hebrew Bible is unsophisticated: it is no less so than argument on the part of characters in any other narrative literature.[1] But the rhetoric that we find in a narrative passage such as 2 Samuel 7 does not seem to reflect a background of sophisticated rhetorical theory or form, at least of any "rhetorical school" that we are aware of. It is, rather, argumentation of the type that all socialized intelligent humans are familiar with.

Having compared the rhetoric of Hebrew narrative and particularly of 2 Samuel 7 to the rhetoric of N.T. literature, I need to make two more distinctions, both regarding context of interpretation. For the most part, the rhetoric that we meet in the narrative literature of the Hebrew Bible is, unlike that of much of the N.T., not framed to convince the reader (or hearer, if you will) of the text. First, the authorial rhetoric of narrative in the Hebrew Bible—of, for example, the narrative within which the dialogue of 2 Samuel 7 is set—seems a surreptitious non-rhetoric that wins assent by induction, not compulsion (a Taoist approach to rhetoric). Second, what rhetoric we do find in the text often operates not on the level of author/reader (or implied author/implied reader, if you will). There is no overt, sustained rhetorical effort to convince the readership to accept what this or that character expounds. Hence, a rhetorical analysis would not normally appeal to the socio-historical context of relations between putative author and

---

1. Alternatively, I do not wish to seem to advance a case for appreciating the literary "artistry" of Hebrew rhetoric. I accept the judgement of Northrop Frye on evaluative criticism and relegate all such positive assessments to post-critical appreciation, in which I find little to value. See the essay, "On Value-Judgments," in *The Stubborn Structure: Essays on Criticism and Society* (Ithaca, NY: Cornell University Press, 1970) and B. Herrnstein-Smith, *Contingencies of Value: Alternative Perspectives for Critical Theory* (Cambridge, Mass.: Harvard University Press, 1988).

audience as a context within which to interpret the rhetoric of the narrative, such as we can and do with N.T. literature. The rhetoric in 2 Samuel 7 has its influence *within* the narrative world wherein it comes to expression.[1] The issues addressed by God's speech in 2 Samuel 7 are issues of the moment, concerns that he and David share at that particular point in the developing story. Our rhetorical analysis should, in the first instance, address them as such. This entails, for example, that when God finally allows that a temple may be built in the future, "for my name," (v. 13) rather than allowing a temple "for me to dwell in" (v. 5), we ought to take this as a distinctive feature of the divine point of view rather than as a betrayal, in v. 13, of some characteristic Deuteronomistic way of viewing the temple (so, e.g., McCarter, 1984:226). The shift is meaningful in the context of Yahweh's speech: he, himself, will not be contained by David, but he will let David's descendent build a memorial building.[2] Such a reading strategy should have a dramatic affect on our reading of the chapter, on the relative positions of the Davidic and Sinaitic "covenants," and on what Cross has called the central problem of the Dtr narrative: the contradiction between what God promises David and the end of the dynasty in 2 Kings. In sum, the rhetoric within the narrative might be read best as character, not authorial argument.

The distinction between authorial and character rhetoric leads directly to a second. My interest in the rhetoric in 2 Samuel 7 is not a study of rhetoric within a known social context; it is, rather, a study of the rhetoric in a known narrative context. The new rhetorical criticism in N.T. studies is much concerned to study the literary rhetorical remains of the text in the context of social history (Mack 1990:13–14, 93–102). Though it is conceivable to try to situate the arguments in 2 Samuel 7 as rhetorical stances within Israelite society, that is not my concern. The two positions in this chapter do not come forth on their own, but as an inseparable dyad in a textual subspace of mutual

1.   At least this is where it ought to remain in effect. It seems that because this book is the Bible, accepted as Scripture, readers feel compelled to allow character rhetoric, especially divine character rhetoric, to move them along with its intended target within the narrative.

2.   Thus 2 Sam 7.13a should not be assumed into the so-called Deuteronomistic name theology, not at least without arguing that the supposed name theology is congruent with and a necessary supplement to the divine character's rhetoric here. But if the latter, how the former?

gravitational influence. What David proposes sparks God's rebuttal and what God advances provokes David's careful qualifications. Before we can even begin to extrapolate social backgrounds, we need to study these views as a pair, in their existing literary context—that, or run the risk of supposing one or another latent social situation behind what begins and ends with God's or David's rhetorical assertion.[1] To put it even more simply: one does not take anything in such a disputation at face value, which is no more than the common rhetorical sense we routinely apply to argumentative communication when we meet it outside the confines of the Bible. When God claims that he has never had need of a temple, preferring the itinerant lifestyle of a tent dweller (2 Sam 7.6–7), we are advised not to be too credulous and, even more, not to go further and suppose the existence, in ancient Israel, of any venerable traditions of the league about a tent shrine that stood in opposition to royal traditions in favour of a temple (so Cross 1973:242).[2] God makes this claim precisely because David intends to build a temple and he wants to cut David off before he gets going. Did God really (i.e., story world reality) never ask anyone for a "house of cedar"? Probably not, at least according to the story that we have access to, but who knows? Is there no truth in argument, especially in argument in the Bible, and more especially in the Bible and from God? Perhaps, but we cannot verify it. What we can verify, what lies before

1. Examination of putative relations between character perspective vis-a-vis authorial perspective must be, at first, put aside to avoid the confusion of voices when we are struggling simply to grasp the overt sense of the rhetoric within the piece of literature. Adele Berlin (1990:563–64) rightly pinpoints the difficulty of making absolute distinctions between characters and authors, as though never the twain might meet. They might indeed, but there is more than enough work yet to do on the first level of rhetoric in the Bible. How can we build a reliable understanding of the nexus of authorial and character rhetoric when we have hardly begun to work on the latter in a clear, self-conscious rhetorical analysis? If anything, rhetorical analysis ought to be gun-shy on account of all the false equations that have come— and gone—in historical-critical analysis.

2. Cross's assertion that the historicity of Nathan's oracle is guaranteed by its context, with which it is in tension, is puzzling (p. 243). In the oracle, God asserts his divine right over and against David's royal right. Such has been and will remain God's habit throughout the entire narrative about the monarchy. The oft-cited "contradiction" in v. 13a, in which God decrees that a son to build a house, fully preserves the divine initiative, which is also supported by the distinction of a house, "for my name."

us, is the fact that God's assertion is provoked by David's intimation, which is disagreeable to God. Rhetorical study, therefore, should have its beginning, and for awhile its end, with an argument in its textual setting. The distinction, then, between the analysis of rhetoric *within the narratives* of the Hebrew Bible and such rhetoric as we find in a N.T. book like the Epistle to the Romans is that for the former the appropriate social context within which the rhetoric must be read is the social context *within the story world*; for the latter it may[1] be the social context between the N.T. authors and their audiences (cf. Wuellner 1987:453, 461–63).

PRELIMINARIES

We begin with three questions:

why does David want to build a temple?
why does God try to stop him?
how does God try to stop him?

These are fundamental questions that face any reader: rhetorical study is just a methodical way to get answers to them. David's response to God (vv. 18–29) is no more than the continuation of the purpose he expresses already in v. 2, adjusted in accord with God's rebuttal (vv. 5–16). If David's intimated bid to build—he leaves it implicit, it seems, because it is a move to gain some control over the deity (cf. McCarter 1984:227)—displeases Yahweh so much, why wouldn't a simple "No!" do? He is, after all, God, and David his humble minion. Why elaborate? The answer to the first question can be gained by studying David's progress to the throne, especially as recorded in 2 Samuel 1–6. The answer to why God would want to stop him may be answered once we understand David's motivation and Yahweh's perception of the implications of temple building. Last, the answer to how God tries to stop David may be gained by careful study of divine rhetoric in vv. 5–16.

The most conspicuous feature of God's speech is its length: it is rare, especially at this late stage in a story that begins in the book of *Genesis*, for God to say so much in response to the actions of a human

---

1. Burton Mack notes that even for N.T. rhetorical analysis, the development from textual analyses to the more hypothetical work on social setting is just beginning and that it is too early in the development of this method to expect elaborate social reconstructions (1990:24). So much the more so for rhetorical analysis of the Hebrew Bible.

character.[1] In fact, God will only speak at such length five more times before the story's end.[2] Something in David's proposal is extraordinarily troublesome for God. The arrangement and style of God's speech, viewed in the light of David's plan for a temple, should let us see what it is that God tries to do with these words. Most certainly we should not read it as belabouring the obvious: the fact that he, Yhwh, would never be contained in a temple is (conventionally) obvious and not needing demonstration. Reminders of his itinerant lifestyle are just part of his rhetorical strategy: he would no more be contained in a tent than a temple. So why dredge up so much of the past when he can just say no?

DEFINING THE RHETORICAL UNIT

In this case delineation is a simple task. David makes two speeches; Yahweh one. David's first speech is complete in v. 2. God's speech is also easy to define: it begins in v. 5 and ends in v. 16. At each end (vv. 4 and 17), descriptive passages from the narrator bracket it. Finally, David's response to the divine rebuttal stretches from v. 18 to v. 29. It too is contained within narratorial exposition: the transitional v. 17 and the opening of ch. 8, an extensive narratorial description of the king's subsequent conquests.

The narratorial material in ch. 7 is slight: the narrator stands aside and reports the speeches more or less as expressed. This is a battle of wits without intrusive exposition: the authorial point of the chapter is to portray the dialogue between the two. The contestive interaction is itself the best commentary possible (at least the best in the eyes of the author who chose to leave it so unadorned of expositional guidance) on future relations and interactions between God and king, between the royal house and the heavenly throne. The absence of narrative exposi-

1. See R.E. Freedman's work on the thematic withdrawal of God in biblical narrative (1987).

2. In 2 Sam 12.(1–4)7–12, Nathan's oracle against David; in 1 Kgs 9.3–9, God's response to the completed , dedicated temple; in 1 Kgs 11.31–39 Ahijah, claiming to speak for Yhwh [confirmation from the narrator comes in 1 Kgs 12.15] speaks to Jeroboam about taking the reigns of power from Solomon; in 1 Kgs 14.7–16, a prophecy through Ahijah against Jeroboam; in 2 Kgs 19.20–34, a word of Yhwh, through Isaiah, to Hezekiah about Sennacherib king of Assyria (a long poetic passage that seems a quote from somewhere else).

tion forces a reader to turn to context and setting as a guide for inter-preting what is said.[1]

Each speech is unified within itself. David's first speech is a simple pair: 'I have a house; the ark sits in a tent.' The binary opposition im-plies that the disparity needs resolving: the ark should have a house too.[2] At first the speech seems a torso, without beginning or end, but it is actually more like head and feet ('I have a cedar home: the ark does not') lacking a torso.[3] Of course the torso is there, only implicitly: 'I would make a house like mine for the ark.' By Aristotle's polemically spartan standards, a speech must make a statement and support it with an argument (*Rhetoric* 1414a 30): David's first speech is an elegant, simple form.[4] Its statement is the disparity in "living standards"; the ar-gument is the implication that the disparity should be rectified, pre-sumably by David.

Critics mostly find disunity in Yahweh's rebuttal. First God rejects a temple (vv. 5–7), then he allows one for the future (v. 13); first he ad-verts to the Sinaitic model of covenant relations, then he undercuts Sinai with the new "Davidic covenant" (see especially M. Tsevat 1980:112–16).[5] Without doubt the argument is serpentine, but that may be part of the divine strategy for revising David's plan.

1. Cf. G. von Rad, "this scrupulous refraining from any direct judgment as he describes extremely moving events, and this imperturbable acceptance of things as they were, moves the reader to ask all the more insistently what the historian's own view was" (1962:313–14).

2. No one, to my knowledge, has advocated the other logical possibility, that David wants to return to life in a tent. Of course, from the divine point of view, that would have been a perfect response, return to the wilderness and all. But David is far from perfect.

3. In the *Phaedrus* Socrates demands that any good discourse ought to have matching head, feet, and torso to make the organic unity that lives and is effective (264c).

4. Literary analyses need not resort to the apology that one often finds on behalf of biblical style and rhetoric. The text may be artistic; it may also fit within the sub-lime, sophisticated, or any number of approbative categories. But it is unnecessary to elevate the status of the literature in order to justify a "literary" or rhetorical ap-proach to it. Disunity and bad rhetoric are possibilities that need not lead inevitably back to the path of literary history. Moreover, we lack any well-founded standards by which to evaluate biblical Hebrew rhetoric.

5. McCarter summarizes the arguments for and against disunity (1984:210–17). I will not duplicate them here. My analysis of the speech's rhetorical unity depends

The speech does have formal unity. It begins and ends with talk of houses and has a turning point in the middle (v. 11b) that modulates the discussion from talk of a divine house (v. 5) to talk of a Davidic house (v. 16). The mid-section treats a variety of concerns, superficially disparate but all connected overwhelmingly to the theme of covenantal obligation: who has been and who will be obliged by whom? The speech hinges at a pivot in v. 11b. Verses 5–11a are organized chiastically as are vv. 13–16. The centre of vv. 5–11a is v. 8a. These verses revolve round the elevation of Yahweh, the belittlement of David, and therewith on reminding David of Israel's and his own covenantal obligation to Yahweh (the structure is outlined in Figure 4, p. 27). Verses 13–16 centre on vv. 14–15 and the consequence of crime and punishment within the Davidic house; they also contain a special contrastive comparison with the punishment meted out to Saul. Together, the topical emphasis of vv. 5–11a and that of vv.11b–16 make a unified statement about divine sovereignty and the obligation of the Davidic house. This statement is, of course, muted by the dissonance between the blasting rebuttal and the blaring dynastic promise, a dissonance aimed precisely at astounding David. His unworthiness couldn't be clearer, the gifts more benevolent, the impact more calculated to stupefy. And that is what it does.

The unity of David's reply has never been widely questioned. It too is roughly chiastic in organization. The centre point lies between vv. 24–25, which are set as complementary parallels. The parallel's significance is much the same as the topical focus of the whole response: as God once established Israel for his people "for ever" (*'ad-'ôlām*) he ought now to establish the Davidic house "for ever." As God was once magnified for what he did for Israel, so now his name will be "enlarged" by what he does for David (v. 23 // v. 26). The speech brackets its central topic—parallels between this moment's "mighty deed" and those of yore, born along on continual encouragements to carry it through—with opening and concluding statements that publish David's admission of his obligation as servant to Yahweh as lord. Thinking to have chanced upon something far better than whatever he had hoped to gain by the temple, David reaffirms fealty to Yahweh. The reply, a gushing glorification of the divine plan, is seeded with winsome suggestions about how God will also gain from it.

on formal rhetorical criteria and an analysis of the argument, a very different approach from the taxonomical content analyses of redactional studies.

DEFINING THE RHETORICAL SITUATION:
NARRATIVE AND NARRATIVE WORLD CONTEXTS

A rhetorical situation is something that a character might try to influence by addressing it in speech. To understand such speech we need to know what provoked it. Everyone knows that comments taken out of context are usually misconstrued. Misquotation is daily fare in discourse situations where a speaker seeks to encourage rejection of argument fragments so quoted. The prevailing circumstance of an argument, the specific condition or circumstance that evoked an utterance, is a necessary context for understanding its logic and structure (Mack 1990:15; Wuellner 1987:455).

THRONE BUILDING:
THE CONTEXT FOR DAVID'S FIRST SPEECH

The preceding context in 2 Samuel shows David setting about the business of becoming king, both as recipient of what chance/God brings him (ch. 1; 3.6–12, 17–27; 4.1–8; 5.1–3, 10–12, 19–25) and as one who hunts down his destiny (2.1–7; 3.1–5, 13–16, 28–39; 4.9–12; 5.6–9, 13–17; ch. 6; 7.1–2).[1] The rivals are out of the way, the people have acclaimed David as king, and the ark of God has been brought to the city of David (2 Sam 6.12). The installation of the ark in a temple built by the king will be the keystone for David's monarchy.[2]

---

1. Cf. McCarter (1984:64–65, 89–90, 120, 175–76; B. Levine 1987:202, 212). Jan Fokkelman's analysis of the structure of 2 Sam 2–5 shows how the focal point of these chapters is the concentration of power in the hands of David (1990:21). David Gunn's thematic analysis of David's story reveals a predominating theme focusing on "giving and taking" in the life of David (1978:95). Gunn suggests, "it is when David's mode of action is most attuned to giving that he is most successful. His grasping (especially in the Bathsheba scene), on the other hand, brings in its train a series of disasters in both political and private spheres" (p. 95). The temple project is an interesting case of ostensive giving combined with a covert bid for power and control. From the perspective of God in the story, it is unfortunate that David chooses a path that must be cut short.

2. No doubt some will properly object, on the basis of 2 Sam 2.4 and 5.3–5, that David has already been twice acclaimed and is in full monarchic control over Israel. But the exigency of this rhetorical situation is not some objective reality (which we perceive only through the filter of the narrative) but David's own perception of it, i.e. his psychological apperception.

BRINGING THE ARK TO JERUSALEM

What David does with the ark in 2 Samuel 6 is an important context
for interpreting his rhetoric in 2 Samuel 7. Until God dissuades him,
the ark is the focus of his attention in both chapters. In 2 Samuel 1–5
David goes about the business of securing his throne, but only from
chs. 6–7 do we get any insight into his plans for including God and
"religion" in his administration. The kingship sewn up (5.10, 12, 13,
25; cf. McCarter 1984:175), David makes a public show of the deity's
approbation for king and royal city and, implicitly, seeks a stronger
hold on the ark and perhaps on the deity too. The incident in 6.7 and
its parallelism with 1 Sam 4 show already that God will brook no
triflers. 2 Sam 6.9 gives a slim but revealing glimpse into David's motives: "how can the ark come up *to me*" (*'êk yābô' 'ēlay 'ªrôn yhwh*)?
David wants the ark not for its or anyone else's benefit: having it in
Jerusalem suits the royal ambition.[1] When his plans go awry, he dumps
the now undesirable ark in no less a household than "servant-of-Edom,
the Gittite" (ObedEdom). What kind of way is that to treat this holy,
venerable object?[2] Yhwh counters David's presumption and makes a
show of his own license by blessing the foreigner's household (v. 11).
As soon as David hears of it he fetches the ark. So doing, David seems
to heal (or more important, is allowed to heal) the rift that had opened
between God and Israel over the ark in 1 Sam 6.20. There the
BethShemites had said, "and unto whom shall he go up from upon us"
(*we'el–mî ya'ªleh mē'ālēnû*); finally David goes and "brings up the ark of
God from the house of ObedEdom [to] the city of David" (*waya'al
'et-'ªrôn hā'ªlōhîm mibbêt 'ōbed 'edôm 'îr dāwid*, 6.12). Throughout the
journeys of the ark, from the Philistines (1 Sam 4–6) to the royal city,
Yahweh makes it clear that he will not be manipulated through the ark
and will countenance no trespass against it. David, unlike the people of

---

1. Of course, one may identify the king's and his subjects' interests as a common good. Sociological approaches to the rise of the monarchy, for example, say
that legitimation of the king was as necessary to the well-being of subjects as it was
to the king (e.g., C. Meyers 1987:362–63). But the biblical narrative of these
incidents is far from a "dispassionate" sociological treatise. What is at issue here is
the wrangling of God and king as each tries to determine the theo-political ordering
that will be Israel.

2. McCarter (1984:170,) discusses the Chronicler's response to this odd choice
of caretaker for the ark. He highlights the incongruity from a historical perspective.

BethShemesh, seems not to learn this lesson from his own experience with it.

More of David's plan for the ark surfaces in the description of what he does with it when he gets it to Jerusalem. The description of "enshrining" (*yṣg*) the ark in the tent that David "staked out" (*nṭh*) for it is odd. "*Yṣg* is a "vivid and forcible synonym of *śm*" (*BDB* §426c). The ark is put "in its place" (*bimqômô*), as though the tent that David "staked out" (*nṭh*) were its proper place and the tent so meticulously engineered by divine revelation and built by no less than Moses were not (cf. Exod 25–31; 35–40). There doesn't seem to be any backward allusion in these vocabulary choices, except perhaps the contrast between David's rudimentary setup compared to that decreed and executed by Moses in the book of Exodus. Certainly all of the sacral precautions required by Yahweh in the book of Exodus are lacking. The primary application of these odd vocabulary choices is a forward reference. Yahweh picks this vocabulary to make a specific point: he turns the language of 6.17 back, away from its application in David's treatment of the ark here and toward an application describing a covenantal act of beneficence performed by Yahweh on behalf of his people.

The implicit proposal to build a house of cedar, like unto the king's, is only the last in a series of stages that brings the ark from the folds of the tabernacle to the "folds" (*yᵉrîᶜâ*, 7.2) of the tent that David pitches and finally into a cedar house modelled on that of the king.

POLITICAL IMPLICATIONS OF TEMPLE BUILDING

One important piece of contextual information is the significance of temple building in the A.N.E. This background is absent in the narrative but present in the cultural background to the king's desire to build a temple. When a king built a temple it not only sanctioned his reign, he being the one chosen by the deity to perform this valuable service to god and society (cf. H. Frankfort, 1948:269; B. Halpern 1981:19–31; Meyers 1987:364), but, inversely and if granted by the god (cf. Ishida 1977:85), it also gave him a form of direct control over the cult and the deity (cf. McCarter 1984:227; W. Brueggemann 1990:254).[1] In addi-

---

1. According to Eckhard von Nordheim (1977:447–48), 2 Sam 7 records the main battle between the ideology of A.N.E. kingship and the covenantal traditions of Israel. The outcome of the chapter is a compromise between the expedient political model and the higher ideals of Yahwism. David's bid to build follows the

tion, it was normal for the palace and temple to adjoin in one architectural complex, giving the king direct influence on the quotidian operations of the temple (cf. McCarter 1984:227).[1] Such an arrangement is manifest in the subsequent description of Solomon's temple construction project (1 Kgs 6–7).[2] If David's desire to build a temple is the provocative context for God's rebuttal, it is also clear that David's subtle proposal is an argument for stability made by a king who has just come to power in the context of political division and instability in Israel. David's need to tighten his grip on power is the exigency[3] that provokes the chain of rhetorical moves in Yahweh's and David's speeches in 2 Samuel 7.

Retrospective textual confirmation for taking this cultural context as the backdrop to David's request comes in the form of the surprising vehemence of Yahweh's rejection. When David comes forward with his proposal, though he is not exactly forthcoming about his political aspirations, anyone aware of the conventional meaning of temple construction, God included, can guess what he is up to (cf. M. Ota 1974). If God's speech is the rebuff that almost every published reading has said

A.N.E. precedent; Yahweh's response represents the ideological response of Yahwism to that necessary development within the Israelite polity.

1. The debate about whether Solomon's temple functioned more as a royal chapel than as a temple for the nation [or world according to C.H. Gordon (cited in Th. A. Busink, 1970:619)] is not the issue here (on the debate see the thorough review by Busink [pp. 618–37]. Given the primary aim, however, it would make most sense for the temple to have the widest possible human clientele, thus increasing the number of those who might avail themselves of the enshrined deity and support the king who provided the opportunity of such service.

2. Such purposes for the temple are evident in the description of what Solomon does and says regarding the temple that he builds. In 1 Kgs 6.1–10 the narrator describes the construction of temple and palace in similar terms: a mark of their parallel purpose in Solomon's regime (cf. S.J. De Vries 1985:103). And in Solomon's prayers in 1 Kgs 8, the single most extensive biblical piece on a king's view of the function and role of the temple, it is clear that the temple itself is a way to gain control over Yahweh (cf. Eslinger 1989:158).

3. Kennedy, citing Bitzer, defines the exigency of a rhetorical situation as "a situation under which an individual is called upon to make some response: the response made is conditioned by the situation and in turn has some possibility of affecting the situation or what follows from it" (1984:35). Cf. McCarter (1984:224), "There was, in other words, an ancient and widely understood association between a king's erection of a temple to a particular god (or gods) and the hope for divine sanction of the continuing rule of the king and his descendants."

it is, it is a rebuff of David's effort to consolidate power by gaining a measure of control over the deity (cf. ch. 6 where the task was to bring the ark of the covenant into the royal city of David).[1] In brief, David wants to house God and God will have none of it. Denying David the security of a temple, God offers in its place a divinely authorized guarantee of dynasty. The "unconditional Davidic covenant" is a heaven sent answer to David's insecurity. But is it sincere?

THRONE BUILDING VERSUS OBLIGATION:
THE CONTEXT FOR GOD'S FIRST SPEECH

The narrator sets the scene in 2 Samuel 7 with a description of David "dwelling" (*yšb*) in his house. Both *yšb* and a second term in the subsequent behind-the-scene exposition (v. 1b)—David "dwells" because Yahweh had given him "rest" (*hēnîaḥ*) from enemies round about—link back to texts in the book of Deuteronomy.[2] Both passages present the peace following conquest as a gift that obliges the recipient (in the book of Deuteronomy it is Israel) to Yahweh. Given the many preceding descriptions of David's fugitive life in which the verb *yšb*

---

1. It is probable that David's experience with the ark in ch. 6 is the immediate provocation that leads him to the hope of temple building. With the ark in his cedar box, he could strengthen his grip on the throne at the same time that he regularized access to and control over the central cult symbol of the deity who could act so incomprehensibly.

2. Cf. Deut 12.9–10; 25.19; S.R. Driver (1913:274); D.J. McCarthy (1965:132); Fokkelman (1990:209 n. 4). P.K. McCarter's text-critical doubts about the originality of "rest" for David in v. 1, which are without support in the alternate text traditions, can be laid to rest. He notes that v. 11ab, which is also subject to McCarter's modifications, contains a promise of rest to come for David. Furthermore, it is clear in 8.1 that David does not have "rest" from his enemies (1984:191).

First there is nothing in 7.1 that demands that "rest" attained at that point be rest for ever more. "Rest," like all God's promises, is always conditional, a perilous possession. The promise of rest in v. 11, providing one allows it to David, is nothing more or less than a promise of continuation in that hallowed estate. The fact that David is back fighting as soon as 8.1, just words away from both 7.1 and 11, can be read in interesting ways. E.g., God, seeing how David's idle hands have made room for mischief, puts him back to work (i.e. subsequent to the temporary state in 7.1 and prior to the potential fruition of v. 11). Such a reading entertains a fickle deity, not an unknown quantity in biblical literature, as opposed to the hypothetical construct of a fickle redactor. Certainly the former is more provocative and lifelike than the latter.

recurs as David evades Saul whilst moving toward the throne,[1] it is
clear that at long last David has come to the end of his own sojourn-
ings. He gets to this personal promised land thanks to God's in-
tervention. But the word linkages to prior contexts go back far beyond
David's past, back to the two passages in the book of Deuteronomy.
With these links the narrator reveals that David's success puts him hard
in Yahweh's obligation. It is an obligation painted with the same brush
that colours Israel's obligation in Deuteronomy. It is from such a
position that David makes his bid to build the temple. The fact that
Yahweh, in his rebuttal in vv. 5–16, spends so much time emphasizing
and reiterating David's indebtedness to Yahweh reveals that Yahweh, at
least, thinks that David's purpose is not in accord with the circumstance that the narrator alludes to in v. 1. From Yahweh's point of
view, David's past as much as Israel's puts him forever in Yahweh's
debt. That is precisely where Yahweh wants him to stay (cf. Hurowitz
1992:163–65).

The second important provocation to God, primary from the perspective of causality (efficient cause), is David's implicit proposal to
house the ark (cf. Fokkelman, 1990:208). In addition to the possibility
that this would give David an undesirable direct control over the central covenantal and cultic symbol, the construction would also put
Yahweh in David's debt by the logic of David's proposal.[2] David would
provide for the divinity that which the divinity, represented by the ark,

---

1. 1 Sam 23.14 (David in the wilderness); 23.18 (David at Horesh whilst
Jonathan returns home to Saul's house); 23.25 (David in the wilderness with Saul
in pursuit); 24.1–2 (David in the stronghold of the wilderness at Ein-Gedi); 26.3
(David in the wilderness); 27.3 (David with Philistines); 27.5 (David in Philistine
city); 27.7 (David in exile with Philistines for one year, four months); 27.11 (David
living with the Philistines); 2 Sam 1.1 (David two days in Ziklag, the Philistine
city); 5.9 (David lives in the stronghold (*bamm'ṣudā*; Jerusalem) and called it the
city of David, reversing his fortunes whilst living in the stronghold at Ein-Gedi
(*bimṣādôt 'ēn-gedî*).

2. Cf. McCarter (1984:224) who cites the Mesopotamian record, in which kings
make note of their temple building projects in their petitions for personal reward.
Of course neither the Mesopotamian kings nor David are in any position to make
demands on the basis of these favours to divinity. The existential gap separating
king and deity ensures that favours so called will always be in the form of petition.
Still the obligation remains, which is precisely why Yahweh, with his own particular plans and concerns for the covenant relationship, will not allow the vector of
obligation to point from himself to David or any other Israelite.

does not have. David has a house of cedar; the divinity has only tent curtains (*bᵉtôk hayᵉrîᶜâ*). Until David voices this request, which turns the tables of obligation on the deity and implicitly threatens divine freedom (of course it is purely implicit and potential, given the infinite gap between David's and Yahweh's ability to enact the rhetorical potentials), there is no exigency to call forth the rhetorical position that Yahweh adopts in 2 Sam 7.5–16. At the least, this is how Yahweh reads it and everything that he says reasserts the old lineaments of covenantal obligation.

A BIRD IN HAND: THE CONTEXT FOR DAVID'S SECOND SPEECH

Little needs saying about the context for David's second speech. God has soundly trounced the initiative of the first speech but seems to have left a door ajar to the implicit personal concerns of David's proposal. David's second speech is laden with the consequence of David's desire to go through the door opened by Yahweh. Opportunity has presented itself and David wastes no time trying to clinch the deal. The prospect of the destitute ark is abandoned in this second speech as David wriggles, in his own small way, to revise and sharpen the conclusive promise that has unexpectedly dropped into his hand. Most important about this context is that it is a situation engineered by God. Whatever the state of David's self-awareness when he responds, whether or not he knows he is being duped and is just making the best of a bad lot, God controls the situation from this point on.

SPECIFYING THE RHETORICAL SPECIES

The concern to identify an argument's rhetorical "species" (Kennedy's term, 1984:19, 36) in rhetorical analysis is much like genre criticism's interest in picking out the genre that has been adapted in a particular literary unit. Aristotle's triple division of these kinds of rhetoric are definitive, though they have been fleshed out by rhetoricians who have identified characteristic sequences or subunits within each of the three Aristotelian categories.[1] The three categories are: polit-

---

1. Aristotle's own critique of a taxonomic rhetorical scholarship is refreshing. Speaking to the subdivisions made within any of the three primary kinds of rhetoric (e.g. in forensic or juridical rhetoric, sub-division into: proem, narration,

ical, forensic, and ceremonial (*Rhetoric* 1358*b* 6). Political rhetoric states a case for or against a certain action and argues on the basis of the consequences for the audience. Forensic rhetoric states a position on a past action and argues the justice/injustice of that behaviour. Ceremonial rhetoric states an evaluation (usually of a person) and makes argument to try and win the audience's adoption of that stance (*Rhetoric* 1358*b* 8–20).

From the start it is clear that nothing that either Yahweh or David say might be called forensic rhetoric. But both David's speeches and Yahweh's speech are very much involved in recommending a particular course of action and its expedience for the addressee. In addition, Yahweh's speech devotes some time dissuading David from the course he implicitly recommends at the outset—to build a temple. All, therefore, would fall into the category of "political," or what Kennedy calls "deliberative" rhetoric (1984:19; cf. p. 146, "Exhortation is one of the two forms of deliberative rhetoric, the other being dissuasion (see Quintilian 3.4.9)"). David's second speech has, in combination with its arguments to persuade God to follow that course that he himself has charted, a great deal of praise for Yahweh's behaviour and stature, past and recommended (e.g. 2 Sam 7.19, 21–3, 28). The second speech, therefore, seems best viewed as an organic unity within which celebration of the deity is bound together with recommendations for the fu-

proposition, proof, refutation, and epilogue [Kennedy's enumeration of the possible subdivisions, 1984:23]) he says:

> A speech has two parts. You must state your case, and you must prove it. … The current division is absurd. For 'narration' surely is part of a forensic speech only: how in a political speech or a speech of display can there be 'narration' in the technical sense? or a reply to a forensic opponent? or an epilogue in closely-reasoned speeches? Again, introduction, comparison of conflicting arguments, and recapitulation are only found in political speeches when there is a struggle between two policies. They *may* occur then; so may even accusation and defence, often enough; but they form no essential part of a political speech. Even forensic speeches do not always need epilogues; not, for instance, a short speech, nor one in which the facts are easy to remember, the effect of an epilogue being always a reduction in the apparent length. It follows, then, that the only necessary parts of a speech are the Statement and the Argument (*Rhetoric* 1414*a* 30 – 1414*b* 7).

Clearly Aristotle's interest is the function of argument and his three categories map three distinguishable situations within which one can state a position and then argue it.

ture in a package designed to curry the deity's favour for the house of David.

According to Kennedy, "determination of the species ... can be crucial in understanding the unit" (p. 36), but his summary suggestions do little more than reiterate the generic characteristics of each of the three types (pp. 36–37). In general, it would seem that knowing the species will attune us, in advance, to the kinds of argumentation and reasoning that we can expect to follow in a speech.[1] There is also the danger that the rhetorical critic might read a speech against its grain in the of a mistaken species definition.[2] Suffice to say that preliminary species definition should be tentative and confirmed or rejected in the course of studying a speech.

1. Of course, we already know these by virtue of having scanned a speech to determine its rhetorical species! Probably the best reason for trying to define a speech's species is that the exercise forces us to focus on certain generic traits of which we might otherwise remain only unconsciously aware.

2. See Kennedy's criticism of H.D. Betz's commentary on Galatians (1984:144–52).

Chapter 2

DAVID'S FIRST SPEECH (2 SAMUEL 7.1–3)

Even though the narrator says nearly nothing in 2 Samuel 7, it is narratorial discourse that frames everything that is said in the chapter and we must pay some attention to the frame as we proceed through the characters' speeches. The narrator opens with David in repose, grammatically and in reality, thanks to Yahweh's activity. The parallelism of v. 1 foregrounds the fact that David's respite is the obverse of Yahweh's activity on his behalf:

Figure 1. Parallelism in 2 Samuel 7.1

The parallel lines open with the same morpheme, "*way*," marking their connection. The first line has the more regular syntactic pattern: verb, subject, adverb; the second is inverted, drawing attention to the contrast within the pair. The king's leisure is of Yahweh's making. The implicit nature of causal conjunction strengthens a reader's perception of the fact that the second line explains the first. David's obligation to Yahweh here is as clear as Israel's in the book of Deuteronomy (12.10; 25.19). This last point is the single most important expositional piece in the chapter: David owes his position in the royal house to Yahweh. Of course this indebtedness is not new to anyone who has followed David's career to this point: what it does is foreground the focal point of the debate between God and David in the first two speeches. By the time we get to David's second speech, the third in the series, the "debate" is over and David seeks only to guarantee for himself what God has offered by way of compromise in his own speech.

David's first speech (v. 2) unwittingly develops the same parallelism as v. 1:

'*ānōkî*   *yōšēb bᵉbēt* ᵃ*rāzîm*
*wa*ᵃ*rôn hā*ᵉ*lōhîm yōšēb bᵉtôk hay*ᵉ*rîᶜâ*

Figure 2. Parallelism in 2 Samuel 7.2

David's personal view is that his position is superior to that of Yahweh's cult symbol. The ironic contrast with v. 1 displays the limitations of the human character's view. The parallelism is identical until the disparate description of the lodgings: the implicit suggestion[1] is that there ought to be parity between the two residences and the probable implication is that the ark's dwelling will have to be brought up to the standard of the king's rather than vice versa.[2] David's argument begins, thus, with a premise that should be acceptable to Yahweh: God's emblem should be treated as well as his human servant. David's rhetorical tack is clear and sound: to establish Yahweh's assent to an incontestable premise and then transfer that allegiance, smoothly and invisibly, to an allegiance to the position that is David's goal: a secure throne.[3]

Typically, for the representation of the character David thus far, we are given no immediate insight into the king's motives: it could be the innocent voice of gratitude (so interpreters from Josephus *Ant* 7.90 to McCarter 1984:196) or the calculating scheme of a politician. Prior context, especially the removal of the ark to Jerusalem in ch. 6, has led many readers to ill-mannered suspicion of the latter. But analysis of the rhetorical situation within which David's suggestion comes to expression supports such a reading. A temple constructed by the king and

1. The "whole exposition is a virtuoso avoidance of the term [temple] which, on the one hand, shows the king's objective best, but on the other is to be criticized severely in the oracle speeches and stood on its head" (Fokkelman 1990:210). Cf. G. Widengren (1952:59), who singles out as the key observation Simon's suggestion ("La Prophétie de Nathan et le Temple," *RHPR* 32 [1952:41–58]) that the primary point of the oracle is to emphasize Yahweh's rejection of any temple. Widengren goes on to suggest that one might read the rejection etiologically: David didn't build a temple because God did not want one (p. 60).

2. The implication of Yahweh's response (vv. 6–7), however, is precisely that things would be better as they were with both David and Yahweh at no fixed address.

3. The analysis of effective rhetorical argumentation is Chaim Perelman's:
"In fact, the aim of argumentation is not, like demonstration, to prove the truth of the conclusion from premises, but to transfer to the conclusion the *adherence* accorded to the premises. Lest he fail in his mission, the speaker should depart from his premises only when he knows that they are adequately accepted; if they are not, the speaker's first concern should be to reinforce them with all the means at his disposal. This transfer of adherence is accomplished only through the establishment of a bond between the premises and the theses whose acceptance the speaker wants to achieve" (1982:21).

housing the ark of the covenant is an obvious move to integrate David's constituents (2.4; 5.3) and to contain the unruly ark and its deity (2 Sam 6). But motivation is not the most important factor here, at least not if our aim is to understand the rhetorical give and take in ch. 7. Whatever David's motives, his action would have the twofold consequence of installing Yahweh's symbol in a house of David's making and thus obliging the deity to David—a single move both obliges and potentially puts the deity at the king's disposal. Yahweh will have none of it.

Overall, David's strategy in this first speech is to exaggerate the disparity between his and the ark's abode while minimizing the covenantal implications of what he implicitly proposes. He lives in a "house of cedar" (*bêt 'arāzîm*), the ark in "tent curtains" (*yeríʿâ*).

ARGUMENT AND ARRANGEMENT: YAHWEH'S REJOINDER (2 SAMUEL 7.3–16)

A chiastic structure links Yahweh's speech to a complex composed of the combination of David's proposal and Nathan's reply. The link foregrounds a jealous deity protecting against any encroachment from either David and his temple or the prophet Nathan and his self-assumed authority (cf. Campbell 1986:78 n. 31).

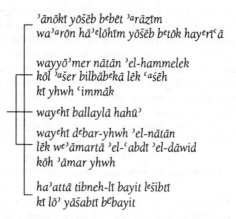

'ānōkî yōšēb bebêt 'arāzîm
wa'arôn hā'elōhîm yōšēb betôk hayeríʿâ

wayyō'mer nātān 'el-hammelek
kōl 'ašer bilbābekā lēk 'aśēh
kî yhwh 'immāk

wayehî ballaylâ hahû'

wayehî debar-yhwh 'el-nātān
lēk we'āmartā 'el-'abdî 'el-dāwid
kōh 'āmar yhwh

ha'attâ tibneh-lî bayit lešibtî
kî lō' yāšabtî bebayit

Figure 3. Chiasmus in 2 Samuel 7.1–6

The turning point in this structure comes at the beginning of v. 4: "on that very night." The narrator would have us see how little time God wastes in putting a full stop to these plans.[1] Both enveloping parallels—between David's proposal and Yahweh's rebuttal, between Nathan's authorization and Yahweh's nay saying, authoritative word to Nathan—show the same pattern of reversal highlighted by vocabulary and grammatical linkages. Such significant structuring, measure for measure counterpoint, typifies the whole speech.

God turns first to David. David had opened his contrastive parallel with an emphatic self-referential pronoun: "*I* live in a house of cedar ..."[2]; Yahweh duplicates the emphasis but the duplication now highlights David's effrontery: "Will *you* build me a house ...?" (cf. A.A. Anderson 1989:118; Fokkelman 1990:208). Where David implied that the "dwelling" (*yšb*) of the ark in the tent was inappropriate, Yahweh rebuts with a simple denial: "I do not dwell in a house."[3] Finally, what

---

1. L. Rost (1982:35 [1926]) observes that the matter of the ark is dropped, permanently, after David broaches it in v. 2, but attributes this to the chapter's literary disunity rather than to Yahweh's forceful rhetoric.

Furthermore, Rost's study misinterprets the entire chapter by using David's second response, "David's prayer," as the foundation for a reading of all the speeches in this chapter (cf. T. Veijola 1975:69–70). His reason: neither form nor content can be used to rule out contemporaneity and thus historical reliability (pp. 35–36; cf. Noth (1957:124), who agrees with Rost's proposed starting point). The generic similarity between David's and such prayers as Gen 32.9–12, 1 Kgs 8.23ff., and 1 Chron 29.10–19 is inconclusive regarding the contemporaneous date that he tried to establish, inconclusive because generic stability is achronological and because the date of these "ancient prayers" is not otherwise established.

2. Similar examples of such emphasis by way of logical contrast are collected in B.K. Waltke, M. O'Connor (1990:295 [§16.3.2d]). Their other category for describing "pleonastic" use of the pronoun is for purpose of "strong emotional heightening" (p. 296 [§16.3.2e], citing T. Muraoka). That too is probably part of David's rhetorical reason for including the first person pronoun: 'I live like a king; the ark (and God) like a peasant.'

3. Ishida says that it is odd that the temple at Shiloh, in which the ark was housed (1 Sam 3.3), is passed over here. His answer is that it would be avoided in a scene constructed to defend David's failure to build a temple (1977:96). Two points can be made: first it is the ark, symbol of the divine presence (cf. Eslinger 1985:166) and not Yahweh himself that is localized in the Shiloh temple (cf. 1 Sam 4–6 where the fortunes of god and ark are clearly distinguished in the story world). Second, God would pass over the Shiloh temple since his purpose is to deny any desire to inhabit such a structure; moreover, his denial is in accord with the notion that the ark, as the name, is a symbolic representative of a divine presence. McCarter (1984:199–200) neglects the possibility of feigned or real forgetfulness on

was only implicit in David's contrast is dragged out into the broad light of full rejection in Yahweh's reply: "Would you build me a house? I do not live in a house." The negative statement of Yahweh's manner of existence forestalls any illusions that David might have had about containing or controlling the deity through a temple complex.[1]

Next Yahweh puts Nathan in place. Where Nathan once pronounced to the king, the real thing is now proclaimed to Nathan. The syntax is identical,[2] but there is a difference: Yahweh's rejection of Nathan's simple saying (*'mr*) takes the shape of an authoritative "word of Yahweh" (*dbr-yhwh*). Obviously Nathan spoke out of turn and not a "word of Yahweh."[3] The rebuff gets stronger in the reversed parallelism of the primary content of Nathan's answer to David and Yahweh's to Nathan: "All that is in your heart, go and do (*lēk ʿaśēh* ...)" // "go and say (*lēk weʾāmartā*) to my servant, to David ...." Nathan's presumption, like David's before him, is turned, tit for tat, back on him. Yahweh's command imposes a potentially humiliating retraction on Nathan. Nathan had granted David a blank cheque to exercise his intimated intent; Yahweh revokes such license by reminding Nathan that David is "my servant." The duplicated referents to David, by virtue of the super-

---

the part of Yahweh when he says that there are only two ways to solve the contradiction: that the editor (?) suppressed a recollection of the Shilonite temple out of enthusiasm for the Jerusalem temple or that 1 Sam 1 and 3 are anachronistic (cf. Cross 1973:73 n. 114).

1. A.A. Anderson (1989:118) quotes, with approval, Whybray's assertion that the dynastic oracle is "the foundation document of David's dynasty" and that leads him to agree that the rejection, in vv. 5–7, of the temple project cannot be a part of the oracle. I agree that the oracle is intended to be constitutional for the dynasty, but not in the way that David, Whybray, or Anderson might think. The whole point of the emphatic and contrasting pronominal references in v. 5 and in v. 13, 'not *you* ... but *he* will,' is that God alone determines who may construct the edifice. The "anti-temple sentiment" that Anderson says is "out of place during the monarchical period" is not out of place in that or any other period because it is uttered by God, who is unconstrained by historical fashions.

2. G.W. Ahlström's suggestion (1961:120–21) that Nathan is the fictionalized voice of an anti-temple Jebusite force in Jerusalem ignores the specific attributions in the text and neglects the implication of this structural parallelism entirely.

3. According to Ishida (1977:94), "Scholars have been mystified by Nathan's inconsistent attitude." A careful distinction between the character voice of Nathan and that of God demystifies the problem. Cf. Heinz Kruse, "What he [Nathan] immediately offered (2 Sam. vii 3) was his opinion, not a prophecy" (1985:147; Rost 1982:56 [1926]).

fluity of the reference, highlight the equation "David = my servant"[1] and carry the implication that he shall do the will of his master, not "whatever is in his heart." Finally, where Nathan assures David that "Yahweh is with you" (*kī yhwh ʿimmāk*) Yahweh places his assonantal seal of authority (*kōh ʾāmar yhwh*). Nathan's assurance of divine support can hardly stand against such a nay saying proclamation.

The structural implications of Yahweh's opening remarks show very clearly that David's proposal is totally unacceptable. The adumbration of divine concerns marks the issues to be treated in detail: in the theocratic context in which David, Nathan, and Yahweh interact, Yahweh alone may initiate any action that bears upon the state of covenantal relations. That covenant is the central issue in Yahweh's eyes is well marked by his choice of vocabulary, which is seeded with terms designed to sound a covenantal register.[2] Standing adamant, Yahweh will not be contained or constrained by a temple.

YAHWEH'S REJOINDER: FIRST SECTION (2 SAMUEL 7.5–11)

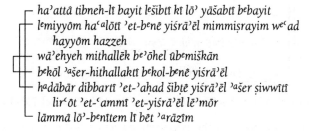

Figure 4. Yahweh's Speech, First Panel (2 Samuel 7.5–7)

---

1. "The name David is now merely an apposition for identifying the servant. David is seen as the obedient one who knows that the norm is above and beyond him in the God he must follow" (Fokkelman 1990:214). I agree that the apposition frames David as Yahweh's servant, but this is what Yahweh wishes to emphasize, not what David necessarily is and not how readers see him behaving. It is a corrective characterization and its intended audience is Nathan, who is reprimanded for forgetting David's servant status.

2. E.g., *ʿabdī* (v. 5); *ʿlh, miṣrayim, ʾōhel* ... *miškān* (v. 6); *ʿammī* (v. 7); *ʿabdī, ʿammī* (v. 8); *ʾehyeh ʿimmᵉkā, ʾakritā ʾet kol-ʾōyᵉbeykā mippanᵉkā* (v. 9); *śamtī māqōm laʿammī* ... *ûnᵉtaʿtīw* (v. 10); *ʿammī* (v. 11).

Figure 4 is the first structure entirely within the bounds of Yahweh's speech.[1] It is balanced, within the first topical region of the speech, against another chiastic structure (vv. 8b–11), with which it is linked by yet more parallels. These cross-section connectors tie the two pieces into a unified argument that begins with Yahweh rejecting David's plan to build Yahweh a house and ends in Yahweh's promise to build David a house.

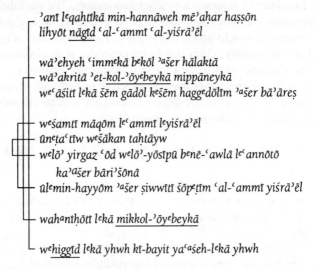

’anî leqahtîkā min-hannāweh mē’ahar hassōn
lihyôt nāgîd ‘al-‘ammî ‘al-yiśrā’ēl

wā’ehyeh ‘immekā bekōl ’ašer hālaktā
wā’akritā ’et-kol-’ōyebeykā mippāneykā
we‘āśitî lekā šēm gādōl kešēm haggedōlîm ’ašer bā’āres

wešamtî māqōm le‘ammî leyiśrā’ēl
ûneta‘tîw wešākan tahtāyw
welō’ yirgaz ‘ôd welō’-yōsîpû benê-‘awlâ le‘annōtô
ka’ašer bāri’šōnâ
ûlemin-hayyôm ’ašer siwwîtî šōpetîm ‘al-‘ammî yiśrā’ēl

wahanîhōtî lekā mikkol-’ōyebeykā

wehiggîd lekā yhwh kî-bayit ya‘ašeh-lekā yhwh

Figure 5. Yahweh's Speech, Second Panel (2 Samuel 7.8–11)

Intervening between the two sections in vv. 5–11 is the pivotal, frame-breaking announcement of an oracle in v. 8a:

we‘attā kōh-tō’mar
le‘abdî ledāwid
kōh ’āmar yhwh sebā’ôt

This formulaic announcement, which signals the end of the rebuke, is addressed to Nathan again. It divides the first section of Yahweh's speech (vv. 5–11) into two parts: the rebuttal (vv. 5–7) and introduces the second (vv. 8–11), a thorough reminder of past covenantal obliga-

---

1. The structure was, to my knowledge, first identified by Fokkelman (1990:215). He calls the unit "the oracle of refusal."

tions due to Yahweh's benefaction (vv. 8–9a, 11a) and a promise of continued benefactions (and implicitly of obligations) in the future (vv. 9b, 10, 11b).

The cross-linked, two part structure of the first section (vv. 5–11) is designed first to disabuse David of any notions about building a temple and then to divert him to the prospect of more covenantal rewards directly from Yahweh. The reverse side of this coin is the same as that of the past covenantal benefactions that Yahweh alludes to. God acts for Israel or David and they become debtors forever. So far as argumentative tools are concerned, the primary device in this section, to be answered in kind when David responds in vv. 23–26, is argument by example: 'these were the past covenantal proceedings and their consequences; so it shall be for an obedient[1] house of David.' Such security for the future is exactly the fix that David sought in his temple project. Yahweh's rhetoric and sequencing of his arguments, Yahweh as villain leads in to Yahweh as benefactor, are right on target as we see when David drops the issue of the temple and moves straight on to the new issue introduced by Yahweh. Not to assume David is a dupe: he may be, but what more can he do than make the best of a godly offer? Still, Yahweh's presentation makes the alternatives that he offers attractive enough that the loss of the proposed temple seems to have little impact on David.

At the centre of the rebuttal (see Figure 4, p. 27) are two parallel references to the past, the way it was (and always will be from Yahweh's point of view). The repetitiveness of the allusion is marked, intentionally so it seems:

---

1. Obedience is implicit in the example, in which Israel's past blessedness is always implicitly qualified by obedience. The logic of invoking an example is described by Ch. Perelman and L. Olbrechts-Tyteca: "Argumentation by example—by the very fact that one has resorted to it—implies disagreement over the particular rule the example is invoked to establish, but assumes earlier agreement on the possibility of arriving at a generalization from particular cases or, at the very least, on the effects of inertia" (1969:350)

wāʾehyeh mithallēk
beʾōhel
ûbemiškān
bekōl ʾašer-hithallaktî
bekol-benē yiśrāʾēl

Figure 6. Parallels in 2 Samuel 7.6–7

The series of anaphoric phrases beginning with the preposition "b" seems designed to impress with the fact that this is a description of how it always was and the collective force of the series is supposed to be more than the sum of the parts (cf. Kennedy 1984:27). Grammatical simplicity is sacrificed to emphatic repetition in the second use of the verb hlk: wāʾehyeh mithallēk ... bekōl ʾašer-hithallaktî. The repeated verb emphasizes the deity's characteristic mobility (cf. A.A. Anderson 1989:120), not a likely candidate to be ensconced in a temple. The parallelism in the last two phrases, bekōl ... bekōl, covers all possible options: 'This is how it was wherever I went and with every Israelite with whom I went.'[1] A key part of this pair and the section is the implicit reminder of covenant obligation that comes simply by mentioning the foundational events in Israel's history. Tent and tabernacle are symbolic reminders of what God has done for Israel. To adduce the example of past covenantal history is to imply that David's proposition contravenes an established covenantal order (cf. Perelman and Olbrechts-Tyteca 1969:356).

The section begins and concludes with an emphatic rejection of David as temple builder: "Will you (ʾattâ tibneh) build for me a house, for my dwelling [when I never ever asked] why have you not built for me a house of cedars" (vv. 5b, 7b). Beneath the near identity of the syntactic parallelism (interrogative + 2nd person verb + preposition "l" with 1st person pronominal suffix + indefinite object + adjective) lies a grating contrast. The contrast, especially combined with the prior contrast with David's "I dwell," (v. 3) highlights the human's presumption.[2]

---

1. Cf. Driver (1913:274), "wʾhyh mithlk expresses forcibly the idea of continuance."

2. Cf. Noth (1957:123, citing M. Simon, RHPR 32 [1952:50]), "Die wahrscheinlichste Erklärung [for the emphatic second person pronoun] is die, dass damit David, auch wenn er König ist, als menschliches Wesen angesprochen wird. Die Veranlassung zu einem solchen Hausbau könnte nur Gott selbst geben, wenn er wollte (cf. v. 7)." I have difficulty understanding Tomoo Ishida's statement that

As Yahweh makes abundantly clear in the second section (vv. 8b–11) David is reckoned among the number of those "shepherds" of Israel (cf. vv. 7–8, (Fokkelman 1990:218)) included in the second "you" (v. 7b) to whom God has never spoken a word about a temple. But Yahweh's representation of the past magnifies the smell of effrontery even more. He makes explicit—"a house for me, for my dwelling" (v. 5)—David's carefully guarded implication that the temple would house Yahweh. The contrasting parallel, "a house of cedar" (v. 7), unmasks David's single enticement by belittling it as something that Yahweh would not dream of. With this pair Yahweh spurns both the idea that he might deign to dwell in a temple, the double "for me, for my dwelling" is emphatic duplication, and David's perception that a god could be as attracted to a cedar home as David seems to be (cf. Wellhausen 1899:254, 268; McCarter 1984:199).[1]

Allusions to covenantal obligations from the past are stronger in the next set of parallels (vv. 6, 7). Yahweh's state of houselessness is explicitly linked to the exodus and especially to what God has done for Israel: "I brought up the Israelites from Egypt." The sense of obligation awakened by the verb *'lh* and the phrase "from Egypt" is yanked into full awareness in the parallel (v. 7). "Did I ever speak one word to[2] one of the staffs[3] of Israel, which I commanded to shepherd my people,

---

the text, here, is ambiguous and Yahweh's reasons for rejecting David's proposal unclear (1977:83). Is the invective by way of sarcasm too far from Ishida's expectations of the divine character?

1. In a section of his study revealingly titled "Wohntempel," Th. A. Busink claims that the Jerusalem temple was, in fact, not an "Erscheinungstempel" but a "Wohntempel" (1970:642). Busink's assertion is part of a larger argument that the temple was not simply a royal shrine, but a national cult centre that benefited the Israelite people as a whole. Its point was to make the divine presence available to all. God's specific point here, in response to David's suggestion, is that he refuses, absolutely, such regularized access.

2. Such a reading takes *'et-'aḥad* (with Waltke, O'Connor [1990:181, (§10.3.1.c)]) as object marker plus indefinite dative accusative.

3. I follow McCarter (1984:192) and Fokkelman (1990:218) in reading *šibṭê yiśrā'ēl* as a metonymy: staffs representing the tribal shepherds who wield them (cf. also, Keil and Delitzsch [1982:342] who cite O. Thenius as someone who reads the word as a metonym for the shepherds). As Fokkelman points out, the parallel between v. 7b and v. 11 is close—in fact, it is part of a whole series of linkages that connect the first section with the second in Yahweh's speech—and supports an identification of the *šibṭê yiśrā'ēl* as the tribal leaders, the judges. Here the short-

Israel ... ?" The chain of command is in full view: God is over Israel's leaders who are delegated leadership over Israel (2 times), over "my people." Both the proper name and the common suffixed noun are emblematic of God's covenantal claim on these people. Without word from the commander-in-chief about a temple, the implication is that there should not now be any talk of it from a designated leader, especially a shepherd of the people with lowly origins such as David's (cf. v. 8; McCarter 1984:198). The comprehensiveness of divine silence about a temple is also underlined by the merismus in v. 6: "from the day...to this very day" (*lᵉmiyyōm...wᵉʿad hayyōm hazzeh*, cf. Fokkelman 1990:218).

Throughout this first section the emphasis is on God's beneficial control over Israel and thus on his covenantal claim on Israel and especially on its leaders. Their mandate comes from God, they take their orders from him. If he is silent about something his people should be too. David's proposal to house God goes against the grain of covenantal history so God continually adverts to the way things have been and to his own role as benefactor. Just as there is an implication to David's proposal there is one to God's rebuttal: Israel (and David too, as one of God's appointed leaders) owes God its allegiance and obedience.[1]

The second panel of the first section centres on vv. 10–11a (see Figure 5, p. 28): forthcoming benefits that will accrue to Israel. As God turns from denial to remind David of the benefits of obligation since the exodus, benefits for Israel as a people are at the centre. Certainly

---

hand expression ("Metonymy does not open new paths like metaphorical intuition, but, taking too familiar paths in its stride, it shortens distances so as to facilitate the swift intuition of things already known," G. Esnault cited in G.N. Leech 1969:153) does more than shorten: it concentrates attention on the pastoral metaphor, which will play an important part in the work of putting David in place in v. 8.

Still, given a free hand to speculate, Driver's suggestion (1913:274–75) that *šbṭy* is an accidental confusion of *špṭy* is attractive from a common-sense point of view.

1. Fokkelman (1990:219) hears the covenantal emphasis in the first section but reads it as emotionally evocative: "God's interest has become plain; the welfare of this nation .... He loves Israel." A count of references to Yahweh, either in the form of pronouns or verbs, finds ten references to the deity and what he has done; there is only one clear reference to Israel as beneficiary of those same divine actions (v. 6). It is not possible to divorce Israel, the receiver, from God, the giver, in the great deeds that established the covenant, but it does seem here that God wants to emphasize his role as benefactor, with the implication of Israel's and David's duty more than he wants to express his tender care for Israel.

there are promises for David too, but they are set in a structural context that aims to remind David that he and his position are literally peripheral to Israel's fortune as the covenant people. The promise of security for Israel[1] goes back to the promises of security issued at the time of the exodus: " I will establish (*śm*) a place (*māqōm*)," (cf. Exod 15.17; Num 10.29; 14.40; Deut 11.24; 26.9; Josh 1.3); "I will plant it (*ûneṭaʿtīw*) (cf. Exod 15.17); "and it will dwell under it (*wešākan taḥtāyw*)," (cf. Deut. 12.5, 11; 14.23; 16.2, 6, 11; 26.2);[2] "it will no more be shaken (*welōʾ yirgaz ʿōd*)" (cf. Exod 15.14; Deut 2.25; 28.65).[3] The final promise, "the sons of injustice (*benē-ʿawlâ*) will afflict them no more," seems to link to a more recent event since the expression *benē-ʿawlâ* occurs only here and in 2 Sam 3.34.

What is Yahweh trying to say? It helps to look back to the parallel turning point (v. 6) in the first panel. There Yahweh stressed his natural freedom as he wandered about with the Israelites "in tent and tabernacle" (*mithallēk beʾōhel ûbemiškān bekōl ʾašer-hithallaktī*). Here, in the second panel, he combines the language of the book of Deuteronomy about the place that Yhwh would choose to place his name and the language of v. 6 about his own itinerant past. Once the parallels have been uncovered, the point is obvious. The party to be anchored to a "place" is Israel; the place to be "established" (*śm*) is that for Israel, not a temple for God (as per Deuteronomy).[4] "Planting" is an

---

1. On the issue of how to read the *wqtl* verb forms in vv. 9–11b see Fokkelman, who provides extensive discussion of the issues (1990:224–26).

2. All of this promise alludes to the statements about the chosen place of worship in Deuteronomy. Deut 12.11 is representative: *hammāqōm ʾašer-yibhar yhwh ... lāśûm ʾet-šemō šām lešiknō*. What God does in 2 Sam 7.10 is to take the commonplace about the place of the temple in Deuteronomy and turns round to refer to the place for Israel. He will not be localized: Israel will be.

3. "Being shaken" (*rgz*) was the fate accorded to the enemies conquered in the exodus and conquest. Israel was only subject to this state, according to Deut 28.65, if it suffered the covenantal curses for disobedience. Yahweh would have David believe that such has been the case and that he now promises to leave off such punishment.

4. Is 2 Sam 7.10 anti-deuteronomic temple ideology? Probably not. Yahweh's point here is to rebut absolutely any notion of staking him down to a sacred locale. The hyperbolic reversal of the deuteronomic "place ideology" is aimed only as far as saying that it is God who will situate Israel, not an Israelite (David) who will situate God. The language of Deuteronomy is a convenient tool (since it treats of the tem-

odd metaphor for securing Israel's place in the land; it links back to Exod 15.17, another passage that describes a localized place for the divinity. Once again Yahweh rewrites the passage alluded to, which speaks of a place (*māqōm*) for Yahweh's dwelling (*lᵉšibtᵉkā*). These things are now applied not to God but to Israel. "Dwell under" is another odd locution that takes its metaphoric cue from v. 6 (where Yahweh goes about in a *miškān*) to adjust the application of the verb *škn* so that it applies to Israel dwelling under the "tent" pitched by Yahweh, rather than to Yahweh dwelling in the place that he has chosen. Topping off this revisionist housing scheme, Yahweh adds two promises of a conclusive respite from the unrest that has troubled Israel from the time of the conquest. The odd thing about this promise is its unusual link back to the promises of peace, which are usually referred to by way of the word "rest" (*nwḥ*; cf. Deut 3.20; 12.10; 25.19; Josh 1.13; 21.44; 22.4; 23.1). This anomaly, like the others in this series of creative allusions, has rhetorical reason: Yahweh saves that particular fulfillment for David himself (v. 11, *wahᵃnîḥōtī lᵉkā*), a boon beyond that granted to Israel. Always as we read Yahweh's speech, we must remember that it is aimed at deflecting David's interest in the temple project while reasserting the covenantal status quo. In that light it is clear that David's "rest" is an attractive step beyond Israel's new-found tranquillity. The last in the series, "the sons of injustice will afflict them no more" (2 Sam 3.34), borrows from David's own public oratory against the killers of Abner, perhaps a subtle promotion of Yahweh's position as akin to David's.

EXCURSUS: A TEMPLE FOR GOD'S NAME/DWELLING

If we trace the occurrence of these two views of the temple through the narrative from 2 Samuel 7 to 1 Kings 8 some consistencies emerge. Only the two kings who try to consolidate their thrones through a temple project dare to suggest that God might be contained in a temple. Even then, David only does so by implication and Solomon backs away from his suggestion (1 Kgs 8.13) almost immediately (1 Kgs 8.17).[1]

ple) for restating the central point of covenantal ideology from God's point of view: divine control over his people.

1. Jonas Greenfield (1985:198) takes Solomon's speech (specifically v. 27) at face value and finds in it a rejection of the view of God expressed in Isa 6.1–5. He posits a challenge, within ancient Israel to the cultic vision of Yahweh enthroned in

Reference	Speaker	temple for dwelling	temple for name
2 Sam 7.2	David	(implicit; cf. v. 7)	
2 Sam 7.13	Yahweh		•
1 Kgs 3.2	narrator		•
1 Kgs 5.3	Solomon		•
1 Kgs 5.5	Solomon		•
1 Kgs 5.5	Yahweh*		•
1 Kgs 8.13	Solomon	•	
1 Kgs 8.17	Solomon		•
1 Kgs 8.18	Yahweh*		•
1 Kgs 8.19	Yahweh*		•
1 Kgs 8.20	Solomon		•
1 Kgs 8.29	Yahweh*		•
1 Kgs 8.43	Solomon		•1
1 Kgs 9.3	Yahweh		•
1 Kgs 9.7	Yahweh		•
*As quoted by Solomon.			

The next pair out from the centre of the structure, but still sharing the centre's focus on benefits to come for Israel, makes a bracket that surrounds Israel at peace with land and leadership, both given it by Yahweh. And these too mirror the arrangement of the first panel:

6   kî lō' yāšabtî bᵉbayit lᵉmiyyôm haᶜᵃlōtî 'et-bᵉnē
      yiśrā'ēl mimmiṣrayim wᵉᶜad hayyôm hazzeh
10 wᵉśamtî māqôm lᵉᶜammî lᵉyiśrā'ēl
7   haᵈābār dibbartî 'et-'aḥad šibṭē yiśrā'ēl
      'ᵃšer ṣiwwîtî lirᶜôt 'et-ᶜammî 'et-yiśrā'ēl lē'mōr
11 ûlᵉmin-hayyôm 'ᵃšer ṣiwwîtî šōpᵉṭîm ᶜal-ᶜammî
      yiśrā'ēl

Figure 7. **Parallels between 2 Samuel 7.6–7 and vv. 10–11**

the temple, but Solomon's declaration as a whole is exactly the opposite—it represents "the cultic vision" at near to full strength. 1 Kgs 8.27 should not be read out of tonal context.

1. "... that they may know that your name is called over this house that I have built ."

Once again the linkages with the first panel guide us to contrasts that are Yahweh's main point. The point of comparison between vv. 6 and 10 is locality: Yahweh has never had one and refuses one now. Instead, he establishes one for "his people" (l^e'amm$\bar{\imath}$), for Israel. His claim of covenantal ownership stands out clearly here, as it does in vv. 7 and 11. In vv. 7 and 11 Yahweh emphasizes the fact that he is the one who dictates to Israel's leaders, whom he "commands" to govern "his people." The connection between these pairs in the second and first panels is, finally, underlined by duplicating the unusual turn of phrase, l^{e}miyyōm // ūl^{e}min-hayyōm. To what end? 'I have *never* been localized ... I have *always* dictated terms to the leaders over *my people*, Israel.'[1]

Third from the centre is a pair (found in vv. 9, 11) without parallel in the first panel. Verse 9 has one pair of internally parallel lines and an anomalous extra line:

> wā'ehyeh 'imm^{e}kā b^{e}kōl 'ašer hālaktā
> wā'akritā 'et-kol-'ōy^{e}beykā mippāneykā
> w^e'āśitī l^{e}kā šēm gādōl k^{e}šēm hagg^{e}dōlīm 'ašer bā'āreṣ
>
> wahan^{i}hōtī l^{e}kā mikkol-'ōy^{e}beykā

Figure 8. Parallelism in 2 Samuel 7.9

In v. 9 Yahweh reiterates past actions for which David is indebted to him; in v. 11 he promises future action that will have the same consequence. The phrase "all of your enemies" links the two verses: in the past they were "cut off from before" David; in the future he will have "rest" from them. The rhetorical strategy is simple: to remind David

---

1. Yahweh is consistent on this point. When speaking to Solomon, once a temple has been constructed, he says "about this house that you are building, if you will walk in my statutes ... I will camp (škn, not yšb) in the midst of the Israelites (not in the temple)." Solomon, needless to say, would have it David's way, with God dwelling in the temple (cf. 1 Kgs 8.13, 30, 39, 43, 49). Solomon's awareness of the ideological dispute is revealed in his opening remark at the temple dedication: "Yahweh purposed to encamp (škn) in cloud; I have, however, built an exalted house for you, a place for your dwelling (yšb) perpetually ('ōlāmīm)." He tries to combine rhetorical contraries the way his father did before him. And like his father before him, he is ignored by his divine rhetorical opponent. God simply reiterates (1 Kgs 9.3), without comment, the "name theology" that he decreed in 2 Sam 7.13.

about past debts and then promise a future filled with the same benefits for which Yahweh is able now to claim obedience. The strength of the reminder is augmented by the allusion to the *Leitmotif* of covenanted divine presence in the phrase *wā'ehyeh 'imm*ᵉ*kā*. Without exception, each time that this phrase has occurred with God as subject it is always in the context of God promising to be with a covenantal partner (cf. Gen. 26.3; 31.3; Exod. 3.12; 3.14; 4.12, 15; Deut. 31.23; Josh. 1.5; 3.7; Judg. 6.16). Divine presence and protection from enemies: these are fundamental to the divine behaviour for which his covenantal partners owe their allegiance. No blithe reminiscence of good times past, David's debt is called.[1]

The standout assertion in this pair has to be the business of promised reputation for David, which sits awkwardly in a context of reminding David about his obligation. What is it doing here and what does it mean? The structure of the second panel as a whole would be more symmetrical and attuned to the apparent rhetorical logic if this future promise were grouped with the promise of future rest from enemies, after the promises about Israel's future well being (i.e., in v. 11). There is only one similar saying in the preceding context, in Gen 12.2, where God promises Abram that he will make his name great (*wa'*ᵃ*gadd*ᵉ*lā š*ᵉ*mekā*). Such an allusion does sit well with the recollection of past covenantal benefaction ("I was with you ...") with which this commemorative segment opens, but its future referent still gapes. One other oddity is that past recollections of God's mighty work on behalf of Israel usually magnify the name and the reputation of Yahweh, not Israel (or David) (e.g., Exod 9.15–16; 1 Sam 12.22). Even David well knows the importance of reputation to the deity (*w*ᵉ*yigdal šimkā 'ad- 'ōlām*) and plays upon it in his fawning praise (2 Sam 7.26). There is no prior occurrence of the phrase "a great name like the names of the great ones on the earth"; this is something invented for the occasion. It stands out here, in the recollections of why it is that David is in Yahweh's obligation, because Yahweh wants to catch David's eye, to show him that with obligation comes a privilege previously granted only to Abram. It also reveals Yahweh's reading of David's bid to build the temple—that it is a grasping after fame, a desire for the stature of the great kings who show their position by building temples for the

---

1. Cf. Fokkelman (1990:222), who observes that the formulaic assurance of divine presence here is also aimed at correcting Nathan's facile assurance of divine support for the temple in v. 3 (*yhwh 'immāk*).

gods. Confirmation of this reading, confirmation that also explains the positioning of the promise of reputation here, comes from the narrator's introduction to the chapter:

A   Yahweh gives David rest from all his enemies
     (*mikkol-'ōy^{e}bāyw*) (v.1)
B   David seeks to build a temple (v. 2)
B'   Yahweh reminds David that he has cut off all his enemies
     (*wā'akritā 'et-kol-'ōy^{e}beykā*)
A'   Yahweh promises David a great name like the names of
     the great ones on the earth (v. 9)

Figure 9. Parallels between 2 Samuel 7.1–2 and v. 9

The parallelism is clear enough: Yahweh positions the promise of reputation as a substitute, one well within the existing covenantal parameters, for the temple. If Yahweh's suspicion about David's motives is correct, this should be mightily attractive to David. And so it is.

The outermost bracketing pair in the second panel begins much like that in the first panel, by emphasizing David's insufficiency to build a temple to house Yahweh: "Will *you* build me a house to dwell in" // "I took you from the pasture, from behind the flock to be designate over my people, over Israel." David's lowly origins, in themselves, are enough in Yahweh's eyes to prove that David has no right to house God. There is a parallelism within v. 8b that promotes the vision of David's lowly origins and the great debt he owes to Yahweh for transforming his lot from shepherd of sheep to shepherd of a nation:

'^{a}nî l^{e}qahtîkā	min-hannāweh	mē'ahar hassōn
lihyōt nāgîd	'al-'ammî	'al-yiśrā'ēl

Figure 10. Structure of 2 Samuel 7.8

David's transformed status—from following "after" to ruling "over", from shepherd to ruler—is due solely to Yahweh's action: taking David and making him "designate."[1] The pastoral motif in v. 8 links back to

---

1. Cf. Fokkelman (1990:221), "Three 'I' forms occur first, so that we do not overlook God's initiative …. The 'I' forms are all parts of predicates focused on David and he is present solely as beneficiary, in the form of the suffix." The argument for translating *nāgîd* as "designate" and a discussion of the strong theocratic nuance of the term may be found in Eslinger (1985:303–9).

the pastoral metaphor in v. 7. It places David in the lower ranks. Whereas the shepherd status of Israel's "staffs" is only metaphoric, David's is as real as the realistic description in v. 8 would have it.

The word *nāgîd* is the key vocabulary link that explicitly ties v. 8 and v. 11b as the outermost brackets in the second panel. The word itself conveys the allegiance that Yahweh claims of David, but Yahweh gives it a promissory twist when he turns that word of obligation into a tantalizing pledge for David's future: "Yahweh declares (*wᵉhiggîd*) to you that he will make a house for you." Should David take the bait, a house for him instead of the one he had planned for Yahweh, God's claim on his "designate" will be doubly indemnified. The one "designated" by Yahweh will have his future likewise designed by God.

The second member of this pair (v. 11b) in itself strengthens the link between the first and second panels: it is the concluding line in the rhetorical question with which Yahweh began: "Shall *you* build me a house for me to dwell in? [No.] Yahweh declares to you that he shall make a house for you."

ha'attā	tibneh-	lî	bayit	lᵉšibtî
wᵉhiggîd	lᵉkā	yhwh	kî-bayit yaʿᵃśeh-	lᵉkā yhwh

Figure 11. Parallels between 2 Samuel 7.5 and v. 11

Rhetorical question is answered with divine decree: "will you build for me // I declare to you"; proposed construction (*tibneh*) with divine fiat (*yaʿᵃśeh*).[1]

Taken as a whole, the first and second panels deny David the right to propose a temple, deny the possibility of housing the divinity, reassert the status quo in covenantal obligation, and promise David and Israel continued future benefit (and obligation) under the existing arrangement.

The overall rhetorical strategy is a combination of emphatic but still implicit recollections of covenantal obligation—Israel's in general, but David's in particular—and promises of future benefit. Everything is designed to steer David away from the idea of a temple by showing him that he has no right to build one and that the same supposed net effect

---

1. Cf. Fokkelman (1990:229), "By using *yaʿᵃśeh* God stands outside the much discussed plane of "I build, you build" and the material object which goes with it; he had already mockingly turned round on such building in the envelope of the oracle of refusal."

can be accomplished by divine fiat. Yahweh's proposition will preserve the pattern of covenantal relations between Yahweh and Israel, but more especially between Yahweh and David.

YAHWEH'S REJOINDER: SECOND SECTION (2 SAMUEL 7.12–16)

In vv. 12–16 Yahweh develops his promise of a "house" for David, explaining what exactly he means to grant. Most important from our point of view as readers is that here Yahweh reveals what he thinks David wanted to achieve by building a temple. As the long tradition of reading the section shows, Yahweh thinks that David is concerned about securing his hold on the throne and securing it, to be specific, from anything like the ruination that Saul suffered. Of course, there is nothing in the preceding context to suggest that such was, indeed, what provoked David's bid. But it is Yahweh's reading of the concerns that David had and in view of David's open-armed response it seems that Yahweh was not that far off the mark.

The history of interpretation of 2 Samuel 7, especially since the advent of a critical readership, shows that the majority of readers have taken Yahweh's rhetoric just as it is addressed to David. The resulting readings are hooked by the same rhetorical strategy that snagged David. The legacy of such bait-taking is the academic consternation over Davidic and Sinaitic covenants and how to explain the chafing between conditional and unconditional covenants. Readers have followed in David's footsteps, so it seems (for David seems as overjoyed by the "unconditionality" of what Yahweh says as readers have been vexed by it), in hearing a new age prophesied in Yahweh's speech. But such reading of Yahweh's rhetoric is too careless, listening, like David, only to the positive notes and overlooking the Sinaitic undertones. David is vulnerable: he has everything to gain from what Yahweh has to offer. Modern readers are not so exposed, though those who belong to a religious community with stakes in a messianism rooted in 2 Samuel 7 may be as susceptible as David. Another assumption that has conditioned much of the recent scholarly reading of 2 Samuel 7 is that it was authored as apologetic literature, or even as propaganda, on behalf of David and his dynasty.[1] Were it such, conditional undertones would

---

1. Carol Meyers, for example, supposes that both the envisioned temple and the tale of its inception might have been used on behalf of the Davidic monarchy (1987:362–63).

hardly be appropriate; but the text must be read for itself before it is read in the light of hypothetical authorial backgrounds.

More, even, than for vv. 5–11, we must stay alert to the fact that vv. 12–16 are the heart of Yahweh's rhetorical effort to dissuade David from his plan back to a position solidly within the existing covenantal order. To use a rhetorical label from modern advertising, Yahweh uses a "bait and switch" tactic. He denies David the sanctuary of the temple, but offers in its place the unending dynasty.[1] But beneath the guise of the dynastic promise lurks the same emphasis on divine freedom (which includes what humans know as caprice) and on the require-ment of obedience from his human covenantal partners as ran through the first section of Yahweh's speech. How does he do it? Why have readers since David accepted what the deity says as the new, uncondi-tional, Davidic covenant instead of as the reiteration, however subtle, of the same old Sinaitic principles? The answer lies in Yahweh's rhetorical subtlety.[2]

God has already used a similar rhetorical strategy in the parallel sce-nario in 1 Samuel 8–10.[3] There it was Israel, in their request for "a king like all the nations," that tried to step beyond covenantal bounds de-fined and defended by Yahweh. They wanted a king "like all the na-tions" to make them a non-covenantal people (Eslinger 1985:254–59). They were provoked to try to become such because of Yahweh's be-haviour in the war with the Philistines and especially by what he did

1. For Rost (1982:42 [1926]) the silence on the matter of temple in the second part of Yahweh's rejoinder raises doubts about an "original" connection with vv. 1–7. Rost's hermeneutic does not allow for characters to be willfully silent about touchy topics.

2. Ishida (1977:95) observes the indirect rhetoric in Yahweh's speech (he wonders why Yahweh doesn't speak with the same directness that he does later, again through Nathan, regarding Bathsheba) but supposes that the strategy of indirection reveals Yahweh's reluctance to dismiss David's plan. In the background, he says, is the Mesopotamian convention that a rejection of a royal temple building proposal implied divine displeasure. "Undoubtedly, the "temple episode" is conscious of this point. It has to explain a delicate situation, in which Yahweh sets David's plan aside, although the king enjoys divine grace" (p. 95). The delicacy is that between Yahweh and David, the former indeed disapproving the latter, but wanting to cut off the possibility of untoward rebellion against the divine wishes.

3. Mark Love brought the comparison to my attention in his thesis, *The Restrictions of Yahweh's Promises to David in 2 Samuel 7* (B.A. Honours Thesis, The University of Calgary, 1990), p. 32.

when the ark returned to Israel (cf. 1 Sam 6.13–7.2, Eslinger 1985:229–32). Yahweh responded to the request for a king first by reminding himself and Samuel how low a blow the request was in view of prior covenantal history (1 Sam 8.8; cf. 10.18–19; 12.6–11). Then, in a series of public proclamations filled with Samuel's rhetorical flourishes on behalf of the deity, Yahweh displayed a willingness to grant their request by putting Saul into office as political leader. Only too late did Israel discover that Saul was not the requested "king like all the nations," but Yahweh's personally selected "designate" (*nāgîd*), unconditionally accountable to God and his servant Samuel (Eslinger 1985:302–309, 348–58). Israel's attempt to remove the threat of Yahweh's irrational behaviour in connection with the ark (1 Sam 6) failed and Yahweh, by means of clever presentation, maintained the covenantal status quo. In the end, Israel remained the people that "Yahweh was pleased to make for himself" (1 Sam 12.22).

In 2 Samuel 7 David tries something similar, at least in Yahweh's view. Like Israel before, David's initiative is prompted, in part, by Yahweh's behaviour in 2 Samuel 6. The parallels between God's action in conjunction with the ark in 2 Samuel 6 and in 1 Samuel 4–6 are obvious; what has been overlooked is the parallelism between David's and Israel's response to such behaviour. David tries, like Israel, to prevent further outbreaks: he just takes a different path. Instead of trying to get out from under the deity, David tries to confine the deity in the temple. David's initial actions in ch. 7 are the direct continuation of what he does in ch. 6: from a moveable shrine (before 2 Sam 6.17) the ark is stationed in the tent that David makes for it (v. 17) and thence, if David's plan had worked, to permanent enshrinement in the royal temple (7.2, 5).[1] Yahweh's manner of dealing with David's encroachment is similar, given variations due to the circumstances of each case. Once again he adverts to the past (cf. 1 Sam 8.8; 10.18–19; 12.6–11) and his sense of Israel's/David's covenantal obligation to him, which he believes has been slighted by David's action (2 Sam 7.5–8). Once again, he seems to grant the petition, but what is given is not what was asked. In place of their "king like all the nations" Israel got the theocratic *nāgîd*. In place of the temple for Yahweh "for me to dwell in" (*lešibtî*), David gets a temple "for my name" (*lišmî*), a formulation

---

1. Of course this means that we accept Yahweh's analysis of David's purpose, "a house for me to dwell in," a reasonable acceptance since David does nothing to deny God's reading of his purpose when he responds in vv. 18–29).

fully in accord with the formula for temple presence that God had set down long before in the book of Deuteronomy (Deut. 12.5, 11, 21; 14.23, 24; 16.2, 6, 11; 26.2).

In both cases Yahweh does and does not allow the request. God's strategy is to seem to allow the request, but only so as to swallow up the potential encroachment on his divine prerogative within the theocratic order and thus to render its threat impotent. In the end, that means disallowing the spirit of the request. In such a strategy lies the answer to the old question, asked implicitly in the Bible itself (cf. 1 Kgs 5.17; 1 Chron 22.8; 28.3), about why David was barred from and Solomon allowed to build the temple (cf. M. Ota 1974). God wishes to seem responsive to human plans, whether or not well intentioned. At the same time he encapsulates and neutralizes such potential threats within the divine scheme of how things ought to be in Israel. David cannot build *his* temple anymore than Saul could endure as king. But Solomon, though a darker shade than David, can build the temple just as David, less an innocent than Saul, could be king in place of Saul. Saul and Solomon are deviations that Yahweh necessarily incorporates into his scheme; the king like all the nations and David's cedar temple are excluded, though their stimulus has an impact on the divine design. By the grace of God it is out of such lop-sided synergy the twisted course of sacred history evolves.

This second section (vv. 12–15), like the first, is based on a structure of enveloping parallelism: vv. 12–13, which are internally parallel (AB:A'B') are linked to v. 16. Within that bracketing pair v. 14 and v. 15 are set as contrastive pairs, the fate of the house of David against that of the house of Saul. Having revealed to David that God would be the one to make a "house" for his covenant partner and not vice versa,[1] Yahweh proceeds to talk about time after David. This house will be a house for the dead![2] In and of itself the wedding of tremendous

---

1. Cf. v. 5; Campbell (1986:78), who labels the reversal a "theology of grace." Kruse (1985:149 n. 22) cites three scholars (A. Guillaume, T. Fahd, J. Wellhausen) who point to parallels in Arabic and Greek oracles in which the item requested provides the spark that ignites a-response from the diviner. Assuming such, Yahweh's play on that convention here is a perfect vehicle with which to turn the tables on David, obliging rather than being obliged.

2. Compare the promised land, as realized within the lifetime of the patriarchs (Gen 23; 49.29–32). The only piece of the land that they own is their burial site (cf. M.R. Hauge 1975:137–38, "a peculiar and even a macabre [tradition]").

promise and the bloom of mortality aims to humble the Davidic cheek. Yahweh's choice of phrasing, to anyone familiar with Israel's best known traditions, is double damnation: "For (*kî*) when your days have been filled and you lie down with your fathers ..." Such words were spoken only once before (by God or anyone else). When Moses overstepped his bounds he was refused the pleasure of the view of the promised land from within the bounds of that most desired place (Num 20.8–13; 27.12–14; Deut 4.22). In Deut 31.14, on the eve of the entrance into the land, God says to Moses, "Your time to die has drawn nigh." Then, in v. 16 we hear the same phrase, "You are lying down with your fathers ..." These are the only places in the Bible in which God pronounces the death of a man with the collocation *škb* + *'im* / *'ēt* *'ᵃbōt* (in Gen 47.30 Joseph uses it of himself and in 1 Kgs 11.21 the narrator uses it to describe the actual death of David). But the allusion goes further:

> *hēn qārᵉbû yāmeykā lāmût* (Deut 31:14) ...
> *hinnᵉkā šōkēb 'im-'ᵃbōteykā*
> *wᵉqām hā'ām hazzeh wᵉzānâ 'aḥarê 'ᵉlōhê nēkar-hā'āreṣ*
> (Deut 31:16)

> *kî yimlᵉ'û yāmeykā*
> *wᵉšākabtā 'et-'abōteykā*
> *wahᵃqîmōtî 'et-zar'ᵃkā 'aḥᵃreykā 'ᵃšer yēṣē' mimmē'eykā*
> (2 Sam 7:12)

Figure 12. Parallels between Deut 31 and 2 Samuel 7.12

The allusion is subtle, more like a private joke than a petite jab at David. For the reader who gets it, it betrays a darker animus behind the light and gushing goodwill of the surface. Yahweh's dying David is a second Moses who to his grave must go before the promised land is gotten. But there is more, a foreboding parallelism between the third lines beginning with the verb *qwm*: the seed *raised up after* David recalls the people *risen up* (after Moses) who go awhoring *after* other gods. Already here, and the intimations will get stronger (v. 14), Yahweh begins to sketch the disastrous course that is Solomon's to take and the punishment that will come down from heaven to meet it (cf. Deut 31.16–17; 1 Kgs 3.3; 11.1–10).

Verses 12 and 13 are linked by topic and parallel structure:[1]

> 12b *'et-zar'ᵃkā 'ahᵃreykā 'ᵃšer yēṣē' mimmēʿeykā*
> 13a *hû' yibneh-bayit lišmî*
> 12c *wahᵃkînōtî   'et-mamlaktô*
> 13b *wᵉkōnantî   'et-kissē' mamlaktô ʿad-ʿôlām*

Figure 13. Parallels between 2 Samuel 7.12 and v. 13

Verse 12b contains a detailed definition of the descendent that will build the temple. The reference to "your seed after you" is common as a way of referring to the continuation of a covenant into the indefinite future (cf. Gen. 9.9; 17.7, 8, 9, 10, 19; 35.12, 48.4; Exod. 28.43; Num. 25.13; Deut. 1.8; 4.37; 10.15; 1 Sam. 24.21). What is unusual is that the person to whom the promise is announced is himself excluded (by virtue of mortality) from the experience thereof.[2] Of course that exclusion fits well with the tenor of v. 12 as a whole. The second restrictive identification, *'ᵃšer yēṣē' mimmēʿeykā*, also links back to the promises to Abraham (cf. Gen 15.4, *'ᵃšer yēṣē' mimmēʿeykā*), where the emphasis, as here, is on the visceral connection between generations of the class *Mammalia* (placental mammals, to be specific; cf. Gen 25.23; 2 Sam 16.11). Why such specificity? In Gen 15.4 God uses this uncommon noun (three times) because he defines Abraham's successor as biological descendent (cf. Gen 25.23; Num 5.22). In 2 Sam 16.11 David uses it to express his horror that the fruit of his own body should seek his death. The logic is apparent when the first and second lines of v. 12 are set in parallel:

---

1. Cf. Veijola (1975:72), vv. 12b/13b form a "ring composition." Rost (1982:42 [1926]), who cites Nowack and Löhr in support, sees it as a mark of duplication. The duplication, he argues, along with the fact that David does not pick up on v. 13a in his response, suggests that v. 13 is secondary. From a narratological point of view, Rost's reasoning, along with the other four points that he adduces against v. 13's "originality," is specious. No "original" parallelism in a literature in which it abounds? Character dialogue must always take up each and every statement made by a conversational partner? Rost himself admits the fragility of such argument, but says that it is confirmed by stronger evidence: if v. 13 is omitted, then God's response, which Rost calls a "prophecy," is single-mindedly devoted to the matter of David's house. Rost does not consider the possibility that Yahweh might have reason to shift focus from temple to dynasty.

2. The apparent parallel in Gen 17.19 is connected to several other occurrences in the same chapter, which make it clear that Abraham is party to the arrangement.

kî yimlᵉʾû   yāmeykā wᵉšākabtā   ʾet-ʾᵃbōteykā
wahᵃqîmōtî   ʾet-zarʿᵃkā ʾahᵃreykā   ʾᵃšer yēṣēʾ mimmēʿeykā

Figure 14. Structure in 2 Samuel 7.12

The correspondences are syntactic and grammatical. They highlight, on the semantic level, the diverging destinies of David's descendant and David. The one, by process of natural mortality, makes his way to the grave; the other, by virtue of divine election, goes toward the fantastic future promised by God. Opposite "*your* days" which are "fulfilled" stands Yahweh "raising *your* seed after *you*"; opposite "*you* lie down with *your* fathers" is "*your* seed after *you* who proceeds from *your* bowels." The last opposition, with David lying with his fathers while the issue of his loins goes on, is Yahweh's starkest dramatization of the contrast between David's fate and that of the forthcoming inheritor of the promise. Nevertheless, though David must die, the expected inevitabilities of mortality are not likely to counterbalance the great goad of secure dynasty with which God tantalizes David. It is, after all, the promise that dances on the surface here.

Together, the last line in v. 12 and the second in v. 13 reiterate a promise of political security for David's successor. The line in v. 13 expands the promise of security, adding "throne" and "abiding" (ʿad-ʿôlām) to modify "kingdom" (mamlaktô).

EXCURSUS: FOR EVER OR FOR AWHILE?

M. Tsevat's arguments against understanding ʿad-ʿôlām as "for ever" have not been refuted (1980:106–7) but his review of the evidence was not exhaustive. The following verses demonstrate usage that suggest a meaning other than "for ever":

Gen 13.15	the gift of the land to Abram
Josh 14.9	the land is promised to Joshua "always" for his obedience, obviously not a promise of immortality for Joshua.
1 Sam 1.22	Samuel, once weaned, is supposed to sit before the Lord "always," again without intimation of immortality.
1 Sam 2.30	the Elides had been promised, in the exodus, that they would serve Yhwh "always"; now "for ever" is at an end.
1 Sam 3.13–14	Yhwh's negative judgement on the house of Eli is "permanent": this does not entail an eternity in hell, only an irrevocable judgement.

1 Sam 13.13	due to misbehaviour, Saul forfeits the chance at having Yhwh establish (*kwn*) his kingdom "without definite term." Saul does not lose immortality; he never had it.
1 Sam 20.15,23	Jonathan binds David (and David accepts) with a "permanent" vow; not an eternal one that David could not keep (nor Jonathan envision?).
1 Sam 20.42	the vow, to be ensured by Yhwh, is "always," but obviously this does not mean to say anything at all about the eternality of the lineages of David or Jonathan.
2 Sam 3.28	here *ʿad-ʿōlām* seems more of the force, "completely, absolutely." David is not protecting his lineage throughout the eons; he is only interested in saying 'we are permanently absolved of this crime.'
2 Sam 12.10	an interesting rebuttal to the *ʿad-ʿōlām* of 2 Samuel 7. Now it is the sword that shall "never" depart (but obviously not for an eternity, unless we have here another anticipation of the common Christian version of hell) from the house of David.
1 Kgs 9.3	Yhwh promises Solomon that he will put his name on the temple "always." There is no eternity here; a scant five verses later (v. 8) he says that if there is any disobedience he will destroy the same temple and that Israel will become a byword among the nations—those who betrayed their god and were punished for it.

There are, nonetheless, occurrences in which "an eternity" or some similar duration seems the best fit:

Exod 12.24	an eternal commandment regarding Passover. However, it is obvious that Israel is not in a position to guarantee eternality here: it means "always."
Exod 14.13	Israel will never again see the Egyptians, whom God had killed.
Deut 12.28	if Israel and its sons keep the commandments it will go well with them "always," (but not for an eternity, because there is a condition attached).
Deut 23.4	permanent prohibition against Ammonites or Moabites entering the congregation of Yhwh.
Deut 28.46	covenant curses to be a "permanent" sign against disobedient Israel.
Deut 29.28	the things revealed belong to Israel "for ever" (more wishful thinking than reality).
Josh 4.7	the stones that mark the miraculous crossing of the Jordan are to be a "permanent" testimony to the event.

2 Sam 7.24	David seems to want to say "for ever" because that is what he's aiming at for himself (cf. vv. 25, 27, in which David adopts the language of cultic praise to suggest the benefits to Yhwh of what David is proposing for an enduring arrangement).
2 Sam 22.51	David again, wanting to claim divine protection "for ever."
1 Kgs 2.33	Solomon, taking after his father, hopes for peace and protection from Yhwh "always" (cf. 2.45, Solomon saying the same thing again).

The citations reveal that only when there is an unusual context in which indefinite term is specifically at issue should the expression be so interpreted. Otherwise, it is best read as signifying "enduring," or some such concept.

————

The repetitions are important precisely because Yahweh withholds these terms from David until v. 16, whereupon it is clear that they actually refer back to the "kingdom" of vv. 12–13 and thus refer forward to a political entity that will exist only after David's death. This contrast is established in v. 12 by itself—a) David will die; b) David's successor will have his kingdom established—and then repeated in contrastive parallelism between v. 12 and v. 13:

V. 12	V. 13
a. David will lie down with his fathers	a. Successor to build the house for Yahweh's name
b. His seed will be raised and his kingdom established	b. Throne of successor to endure

Viewed this way the contrast within v. 12 carries across the parallelism between vv. 12–13. Now contrasting with David lying down with the fathers is his successor building the temple denied to David.[1] The identity of the second item in each verse only makes the contrast between the first items more glaring. Of course the temple to be built in v. 13 is not exactly the temple denied to David: it is, rather, the temple "for my name" rather than "for me to dwell in" (lišmî rather than lešibtî).

————

1. Cf. McCarter (1984:205), "The emphatic pronoun (hû', "*He*") echoes another in v. 5 ('attâ, "*you*"), and the effect achieved is one of contrast—"*You* will not build me a house ... *he* will."

EXCURSUS: VARIATIONS ON READING VARIATION

According to McCarter (1984:205–6) and others, there is an irresolvable conflict between v. 13a, which allows a temple, and vv. 5–7, in which Yahweh's rejection of the temple is absolute. McCarter accepts the common notion that the "name theology" of v. 13 is Deuteronomistic (p. 206). From the perspective of narrative analysis, the so-called name theology is localized and appropriate, in 2 Samuel 7, to Yahweh's rhetoric. The logic of denying a temple to house God but allowing a temple that memorializes the divine name is native to Yahweh's overall rhetorical purpose here: to assert divine freedom, to reiterate Davidic obligation to Yahweh, and to put David once more in a godly gratitude by granting new benefactions, one of which is a temple that supports the theocratic model established by God in Deuteronomy.

So the issue is: why deny God a notion that fits so well what he tries to do throughout his speech? McCarter adduces a comparative parallel,[1] but doesn't acknowledge that the analogy might explain exactly what Yahweh hopes to accomplish by allowing a temple for his name rather than one for him to live in. The contrast is even starker from Baruch Levine's view that Yahweh "insists on a "house"" in v. 13 (1987:212b). But there is nothing in the grammatical structure, especially when Yahweh's speech is taken in rhetorical context, that would suggest that v. 13 is a demand rather than a dissembling rhetorical parry.

The distinction between a temple for the name rather than for a dwelling is, alone, enough to make one wary of the common claim of a supposed contradiction between assent for this future temple and rejection of the temple that David intended to build.[2] Nevertheless, most redactional analyses have tagged v. 13 as a Dtr insertion. Mettinger (1976:56–57) argued against such attribution for reason of the literary correspondence between v. 5 and v. 13. A.F. Campbell (1986:73 n. 21) criticizes Mettinger's reasoning and thus the position from which my rhetorical analysis is made. "The argument is methodologically wrong; the conclusion goes beyond the evidence. It is perfectly possible for a later scribe to style an addition in harmonious correspondence with what is already in the text.... Neither unity of theme, nor correspondence of phrases or structural elements can be held to demonstrate their original unity within a text. Such observations are compatible both with original unity and skillfully competent redactional activity."

1. "The assertion of a king's sovereignty through his "name," a surrogate presence, assured his continuing control of a dominion in his absence (cf. de Vaux 1967)" (1984:206).

2. For historical-critical arguments in favour of the integrity of v. 13 in context, S. Mowinckel's pioneering article is usually cited ("Natanforjettelsen 2. Sam Kap. 7," *SEÅ* 12 (1947):220–29 [cited from the reference in G. Fohrer 1959:10, n. 18]). For a redactional argument favouring the need to be careful about the distinction between a temple "for my name" and "for me to dwell in" see Kumaki (1981:23–24).

Campbell (with M.A. O'Brien) has refined this radical position in a critique of something I had said. In a study of 1 Sam 8–12, I argued that one might read variant points of view as a single exploration, within a unified literary composition, of a problematic issue or issues (1985:38). I suggested that literary historical readings of complex texts (i.e., texts expressing multiple, contradictory views) must defer to literary readings that can make sense of the multiplicity within the literary or narrative logic of the text being read.[1] Only if we approach the text assuming multiplicity must we read complex texts as composite texts. Campbell/O'Brien counter,

> Eslinger skates too lightly over this issue: … If, unencumbered, we approach a text that expresses contrary views, it is legitimate to ask about the origin of these contrary views—authored or quoted. If the text is such as to sustain a hypothesis of single authorship, the origin of the views is a traditio-historical question. In what circles are they likely to have been handed down until they have been expressed by this one author in this one text? If the text is such as to sustain a hypothesis of multiple authorship, with perhaps a single compiler, the origin of the views may be a source-critical question and the answer may be genetic. Explanations of "last resort" have nothing to do with it. Composite texts do not fall together all of a piece; they imply skillful composition of traditions of varying genetic origin to form a text, a process that can take place in a number of ways. The text's reading is then a work of interpretive art" (1993:208 n. 17).

1. Bernard Levinson's recent defense of historical criticism and of the certain gains of a diachronic approach seems to agree on such analytical sequence. Speaking about the flood stories and when it is that one should switch from a synchronic to a diachronic hermeneutic, he says,

> Herein lies the justification for the diachronic analysis of the Bible according to the standard historical-critical method. The two contiguous passages cannot construe in terms of a narrative poetics that derives the text from the artistic genius of the narrator. The interpreter's methodology, to comprehend the text, must consequently shift from a synchronic poetics to a method informed by diachrony, an analysis of the text as the work of a redactor who has conjoined originally separate literary documents (1991:139).

It seems a banal suggestion that one ought to continue reading a text as a single train of thought until one can't go any further, but the proposition of Campbell and O'Brien raises reasonable doubt about the reasonableness of such a hermeneutical strategy, especially for someone, such as myself, sympathetic to historical-critical goals. Levinson's position, I think, is closer to the classical position in historical-critical analysis. It is also more defensible than Campbell/O'Brien's, behind which the spectre of a stuttering hermeneutical *reductio ad absurdum* looms.

Thin ice does beg a light foot, but I agree on the basic point—that the presuppositions with which we approach the text determine our result. Still, I have misgivings. At what point in interpreting a complex text does one make the decision to step through the world of the text, the story world, into the real world in which the text was created? Only within the cloistered reading community of historical criticism does one regularly suppose that multiplicity of representation or contrary views expressed by different (or even the same) voices in the story world might be explained by positing multiple authors (source criticism, redaction criticism) or varying bodies of tradition (tradition history). The ever present pitfall for such speculation is that one will fabricate a historical entity or entities to account for differences that are purely literary. How does one know what is fair game for literary-historical reconstruction and what is best left as literary artifact? It is a fine line to draw, but a glance at historical-critical analyses of the biblical texts (texts that all now agree, however grudgingly, betray a concern for literary refinement) shows that purely "literary" obstructions to a simple reading are rarely encountered. Is this simply an unfortunate consequence of scholarly politics, in which an admission of an exception to the rule of contradiction opens the lid of Pandora's box? A less cynical view is that the method leaves nothing out because all is, in principle, accountable by its literary-historical presuppositions about the text's production history. The same is true, of course, for the "literary" analyses: all but the worst incongruities can, it seems, be explained as integral to a unified text. Both attitudes, then, bear predetermined consequences in their presuppositions. Depending on whether one is more or less venturesome one will favour a historical-critical or a literary explanation of the text.

How shall one choose, then, between the methods? There is a simple way. If one's interest is the history of Israel, or even the literary history of the Bible, one must rely on the historical-critical method (cf. A. Kuenen 1894:6, 14–15) and hazard the concomitant historical speculation. A literary approach, if not subsequently developed beyond agnosticism regarding the literary or social history underlying the literary construction, fails the historical-critical test. If one's concern is to explain and understand biblical literature for itself, then one will be drawn to a literary model. It has the logical advantage of reliance on fewer hypotheses to explain the literary features of the text.[1] Most of all, one only needs to compare a careful literary analysis (say Fokkelman's reading of Samuel) with a careful historical-critical analysis (say Campbell's analysis of Samuel–Kings) to see that the latter is concerned with the literature mainly for its reflection of historical entities beyond. I have little doubt that in the current scholarly community, Campbell's reading of the contradiction between 2 Sam 7.5 and 13 will be popularly found

---

1. I speak, of course, in relative rather than absolute terms. Even a cursory consideration of the endemic hermeneutical problems attending human understanding, not to mention textual comprehension, renders all "advantages" insignificant. But in that order of self-scrutiny, the niceties of biblical interpretation are hardly critical—in either sense of the term.

more interesting and acceptable ("When v. 13 is recognized as dtr, the principal statement about a temple in the pre-dtr text is the prohibition against building one" [1986:73]). But for someone with an interest in the theological complexities that the text seems to treat, the nay-saying Dtr is a dull second to Yahweh's skillful subversion of David's plan.

Beyond these polar methodological oppositions many proclaim a third, synthetic option. It is conceivable that one might do justice to the literary details of the text, treating them as literary features, and then go on to consider the historical ramifications.[1] The priority in such a task, however, is first literary analysis followed by literary history and/or historical analysis. Ironically, such procedure is dictated by the fundamentals of good historical-critical practice.[2] There are several examples, in fact, of such a methodological priority in the field of gospel criticism. Sean Freyne, in his study of Galilee in the gospels, says "there is good reason for starting with the texts that tell the story of Jesus the Galilean, and that not out of deference to the new trends, but in order to establish the proper set of questions for the subsequent historical investigation" (1988:26). Similarly, Herman Waetjen, whose ultimate goal is a socio-political analysis, says that we must start with a distinctly literary analysis. "In no way is it [gospel of Mark] a copy of the world in which it originated, in spite of its reflection of the social, economic, political, cultural, and religious realities of its agrarian context in the first-century Roman-occupied Palestine and Syria" (1989:1). In my opinion, Campbell and O'Brien's point subverts the methodological priority of literary criticism over any kind of historical analysis, and source or tradition criticisms are historical, not literary criticisms.[3]

ANTONY CAMPBELL RESPONDS

A major issue is shaping up in biblical studies over how texts are to be read. Any opportunity that enhances communication between what are fast becoming two camps is to be welcomed, so I am grateful for the offer of a response to Prof.

1. But note the cautions expressed by Edward L. Greenstein (1988:353) in his review of an early attempt at such a synthesis, David Damrosch's "diasynchronic" reading of biblical narrative. Such synthesis is only possible, in my view, once historically oriented scholarship recognizes the fact that literary analysis precedes historical. To try to synchronize the two as different approaches that can be applied as one sees fit, on a level playing field of methodological pluralism, can only produce mutant readings.

2. Cf. M. Noth, "It must remain, or rather become once again, a principle of any sound criticism of the Pentateuch not to assume literary disunity unless the occurrence of variants, of obvious seams and secondary connections, and the like *compels* such an assumption" (1972:24; cited in Campbell, O'Brien, p. 164).

3. See, also, R.G. Moulton's (1908) still unanswered assertion of the methodological priority of literary analysis.

Eslinger. My colleague and co-author, Mark O'Brien, is out of Australia at the time of writing, so this has to be on my own responsibility. I believe a response is particularly important, because I find areas in dispute that leave me genuinely puzzled. Biblical studies is an immense and complex area, like any great field of study. I will focus my response on three precisely defined points.

First, Eslinger quotes me on the literary correspondences between 2 Sam 7.5 and 7.13 (*House of God*, 50). Accepting the correspondence, my argument is that v. 13 may correspond with v. 5 *either* because the same person wrote both verses *or* alternatively because a second person writing v. 13 chose to imitate v. 5. My conclusion: "Such observations are compatible both with original unity and skillfully competent redactional activity" (1986:73 n. 21). This seems to me perfectly straightforward. I am puzzled that it attracts Eslinger's fire.

Second, Eslinger considers that O'Brien and I have "refined this radical position" (*House of God*, 50). Our argument is that in a text expressing contrary views it is possible that a compiler has put together traditions taken from the opposing parties (e.g., Democratic and Republican convention platforms); alternatively, it is possible that one author has contrasted views that would be held by the opposing parties (e.g., conservative Republicans and liberal Democrats). This seems to me perfectly simple and anything but a radical position. I am puzzled that it arouses Eslinger's ire.

Third, Eslinger notes Bernard Levinson's discussion of the flood stories in his conclusion:

> The two contiguous passages cannot construe in terms of a narrative poetics that derives from the artistic genius of the *narrator*. The interpreter's methodology, to comprehend the text, must consequently shift from a synchronic poetics to a method informed by diachrony, an analysis of the text as the work of a *redactor* who has conjoined originally separate literary documents.

Eslinger comments that "it seems a banal suggestion that one ought to continue reading a text as a single train of thought until one can't go any further" (ibid.). With this comment I would have thought we had found common ground at last; it is basic to our work in *Sources of the Pentateuch*. We endorse more than once the quotation from Noth that Eslinger singles out approvingly (*House of God*, 52, n. 2): literary disunity is not to be assumed unless the evidence *compels* such an assumption. So I am puzzled that Levinson is reckoned with the angels and O'Brien and I are menaced with responsibility for "the spectre of a stuttering hermeneutical *reductio ad absurdum*" (*House of God*, 50 n. 1).

This is all the more puzzling when O'Brien and I have given a substantial section to the flood narrative (1993:211–13). We discuss both synchrony (unity) and diachrony (duality) and we do not abandon synchrony. "In the combination of sources, unity almost always has priority over duality. ... Yet duality has consistently been maintained; although not in the foreground, it has seldom been eliminated. The principal conclusion to be drawn from this must be that although unity is the principal concern of the combined text, the duality is also of sufficient significance to be preserved" (1993:220). I am puzzled by Eslinger. Why is this disregarded? Where is the spectre and the stuttering? What is running?

In the end, Eslinger complains that O'Brien and I ignore "the methodological priority of literary criticism over any kind of historical analysis, and source or tradition criticisms are historical, not literary criticism" (*House of God*, 52–53). I endeavour to sail my interpretative skiff between the Scylla and Charybdis of this polarity. I have stated my position elsewhere: "one of the first things to be done in approaching the study of a biblical text is to take an inventory of its phenomena to assess its nature and whether it is a composite text or an original unity" (1989/92:133). In Eslinger's words, this means first trying to read a text "as a single train of thought until one can't go any further."

If the methodological priority of literary criticism is an ideological commitment to the unity of the text, I do not ignore it. I reject it.

Incidentally, for me "historical criticism" is not now about history. It may have been once; it is not now. For me, "historical criticism" is about approaching a text with historical awareness—a very different kettle of fish. I resist being trapped between history and literature; my primary concern is with the theology in the text.

O'Brien and I have a high regard for the competence of biblical editors and redactors, with redaction recognized as "a highly skilled literary enterprise" (1993:17). After pondering the Pentateuch, we go on to say: "The question we need to ask now is whether the intelligence of the biblical compilers and redactors is appropriately valued by seeking out a sometimes unnaturally forced unity on their texts" (1993:206). The difference between Eslinger's and our analyses may well rest on what is understood as "unnaturally forced."

We have raised the question of the purpose served by ancient biblical texts. It is certain that "our post-Gutenberg concept of texts written for distribution to a wide readership was not the case in ancient times" (1993:204). There is a risk that the recent literary insistence on unity may lead us to "unconsciously imposing a modern Western convention on ancient texts" (1993:203). Instead, we are invited to make an imaginative leap as to the purposes served by these ancient texts.

From our experience of the texts, O'Brien and I raise the question "whether all our biblical texts are the final product of literary output or whether some of them are intended as the starting point from which literary output is produced" (1993:208). Do our biblical texts preserve variant views, pointers to variant possibilities in the telling of a story, traditions that are to be preserved or that may be used to enhance or embroider a story?

If there are indeed two camps in biblical interpretation, it may be that they are energized by fidelity to different experiences of the biblical text. For interpreters like O'Brien and me, the biblical text reveals itself as one in which "views are expressed and traditions told, modifications are made, contradictory positions are proposed, composite texts are compiled, prophetic texts are updated, and so on— and all the while, faith is eternally questing for understanding" (1993:xiv). A different experience of the text will naturally generate a different reading. I do not believe it is adequate to explain such different experiences as the result of differing presuppositions. The difference is deeper, even if we have not as yet laid bare its roots.

Antony F. Campbell

24 September, 1993

Prof. Campbell's response brings the issue to a sharpened focus. I am grateful for his gracious reply and will respond and extend, a bit, this opportunity for dialogue. By way of preface, I disavow any intent to express "fiery," "irate," "menacing," or "complaining" attitudes in my comments on the position represented by the work of Campbell/O'Brien. I picked their book neither as a target nor to broaden this discussion to include Pentateuchal texts, but as a model of frank and stimulating discussion of the issues. Perhaps the spirit in which the comments were offered suffered some transfiguration in their reception. What I have said and will say is offered in the hope of cooperation and understanding. I take Campbell's remarks the same way.

Campbell objects to my characterization of his position as "radical," claiming (also in a complementary letter) that there is nothing new about this supposition that a redactor is just as capable as an author of adding a piece that fits with an existing bit of literature. I use the adjective "radical" because this strikes me as about as far as one can go in making room for redactors (a literary-historical rather than a literary concept) in a text that, for argument's sake, betrays no obvious mark of redaction. If an "addition" is "in harmonious correspondence" with the rest of a text how comes one to a redactional ascription? Simply because it "is perfectly possible"? Given such a possibility, which anyone could accept in principle, one could fragment "established" unities such as the four sources of the archetypic documentary hypothesis. I called the position radical, not for its novelty but for its logico-literary possibilities. It bears within it the prospect of unending subdivision[1] of the literature even when the narrative flow might appear continuous. What is to stop another interpreter after Campbell from taking his reading of 2 Sam 7.13 a step further, saying that it is not the unified redactional artifact of "dtr," but rather of dtr^1 and dtr^2, or $dtr^{1,2,3\dots}$? Nothing, in principle, because given this presupposition there is no halt, theoretically speaking, before the literary equivalent of atomism. One can never say "Enough!" because it is yet possible that enough is not enough. Campbell tries to be accommodating by saying that there is room for both synchronic and diachronic analyses, each with a different goal, but perhaps complementary results. Such is the model that he and O'Brien offer in their manual of Pentateuchal criticism. I have no more ideological opposition to such complementarity than I have favour for ideological commitment to textual unity, original or otherwise. But I do think that after one has said that the difference

---

1. Unending—thus my uncharitable image of a stuttering *reductio ad absurdum*. It was not my intent to menace Campbell/O'Brien with responsibility for such unending division—only to say that some mean-spirited person might go through that door and take the option to its logical conclusion.

between 2 Sam 7.5 and v. 13 is integral to Yahweh's rhetoric, the mere possibility that the two verses might represent the contrary views of two authorial hands is: a) insufficient; and b) argument against the original reading of rhetorical suitability.[1] Where Campbell proposes a methodological both/and, I see an either/or. You can't have unified character rhetoric (2 Sam 7.5, 13 is not a case of the more complex issue of authorial rhetoric) and find in it the reflection of authorial diversity. If there is diversity, however oblique, then my argument for rhetorical unity is weakened and I must counter or yield. But facing a simple possibility, I see no warrant for deference.

Neither is it the case that historians can only get where they want to go with Campbell's option. From my point of view, the case is quite the reverse. However much fictionality inheres in what they ultimately create, it seems that historians do their best to strive for accurate representations of history. In view of the atomistic possibilities of multiplicity, the historian must face the prospect that he/she has allowed a glib continuity where an underlying plurality ought to prevail. But worse yet, if the supposed disparity between something like 2 Sam 7.5 and 13 is truly resolved within the fictive context of Yahweh's rhetoric, the historian who pursues pluralistic authorial possibilities pursues phantoms and neglects the historical singularity into which the monodic rhetoric may allow some sidelong glance.

I would conclude with some readerly admissions. My stake in the unity of the text is theologically trivial, but hermeneutically fundamental. Leaving history aside, for the moment as I do, why should anyone, inerrantists aside, care how many hands have had a hand in the scripture so long as it gets them, and it almost always does , where they want to go? Reading the long history of theological reflection that often masqueraded as scientific historical criticism, it doesn't seem that dtr[1,2,3]... have been found wanting, theologically, to those who perceive a multi-layered legacy rather than that of the single Dtr. As for "original unity," literary-historical agnosticism has no more use for it than for "original disunity." The question, rather, is whether the text we face seems unified or diversified. By whose canon shall we decide? A reasonably broad reading acquaintance with the product of biblical scholarship has made me skeptical and agnostic about our grasp of the Bible's literary history. In sympathy with the desire to know it, even with the often commonsensical suppositions about how it must have come about in ways much different than our own post-Gutenberg modes of literary production, I do not find the possibility that two or more hands might have done the apparent work of one a convincing reason to "believe in" the existence of two or more hands.

1. In fact, Campbell's reading of this particular pair of verses may be less hypothetically based. I juxtapose two of his statements: "literary disunity is not to be assumed unless the evidence *compels* such an assumption" and "the difference between Eslinger's and our analyses may well rest on what is understood as "unnaturally forced"." Might it not be a case of differing readings of the literary evidence? If so, I would prefer to set my reading against Campbell's reading, not against the hypothetical possibility of multiple authorship.

Campbell is right to say that there is a deep rooted difference, no matter whether it is called a presupposition or a world view, between the radically polarized "unified" and "dualified" readings. I am as incredulous about his acceptance, for purposes of interpretation, of the possibility of multiple hands behind an apparent unity as he is about my rejection of it as an exegetical strategy. We do agree in principle: yes, this is possible. My reasons for rejection of the possibility are an attraction to logical economy and an acquired skepticism about literary-historical speculations on the processes that culminated in the received text. These are important presuppositions that predispose my reading. From what he has said, I cannot discern Campbell's "absolute presuppositions" (R.G. Collingwood's term) or deep roots or whatever we shall call such constraints on thought.

———

The subtle change in the reference to the temple, from a temple "for my name" to one "for me to dwell in," is part of Yahweh's encircling move by which David's constraining temple is incorporated into the theocracy, albeit in neutered form (cf. A. Weiser 1965:158–60; R. Schwartz 1991:199). The real distinction between David lying with the fathers and the providentially successful successor remains, "for a living dog is better than a dead lion" (Eccl 9.4).

Verses 14 and 15 are the heart of the enveloped structure in this second section of Yahweh's speech. Comparative contrast is the primary rhetorical device: the fate of the adopted but sinning Davidide compared to the repudiated dynasty of Saul. Before the contrast, however, we must look at v. 14, which has its own integral concentric structure.

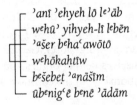

'anî 'ehyeh lô le'āb
wehû' yihyeh-lî lebēn
'ašer beha'awōtô
wehōkaḥtîw
bešebet 'anāšîm
ûbenigᶜê benê 'ādām

Figure 15. Structure in 2 Samuel 7.14

The structural integrity of the verse is primarily marked by the enveloping word pairs: *'āb* // *'anāšîm*, *bēn* // *benê 'ādām*.[1] The point of this par-

---

1. Though the word *'āb* is not an exact parallel to *'anāšîm* it is clear from the parallel relationship between *bēn* and *benê 'ādām*, which share a common noun, that

ticular bit of repetition is to emphasize the notion of a closer, more "human" relationship between the fatherly deity and David's royal successor. But this stress must be read as counterpoint to v. 15, in which the treatment of Saul is the focal point. In that contrast the human-kindness metaphor of v. 14 balances opposite the fated demise of the unfortunate Saul.

The focal point of v. 14 is deviance and its reproof. Yahweh does not say 'if he sins, I will correct him'; rather, he says 'when he goes astray....' Inevitable defection from a divinely observed standard of behaviour is presumed. Whether that be the Sinaitic covenant or simply God's watchful eye is of little consequence. As always, the deity commands an expected code of behaviour and the human partner is expected to maintain it. The fact that the standard goes unmentioned here suggests, however, that it is common knowledge, unless the point were that the deity will arbitrarily adjudge behaviour by a code known only to him—doubtful given that we read, here, the expression of Yahweh's point of view. To describe the errant behaviour and its correction, God chooses a vocabulary appropriate to the familial metaphor to frame his description of future relations between himself and the successor (cf. McCarter 1984:207 citing McKane and Weinfeld). The diminutive terms for punishment have been selected with an eye to the contrast between God's metaphoric fatherliness toward the successor and the wrath that descended on Saul. The "rod of men" for a wayward son is probably akin to the rod of instruction mentioned in the book of Proverbs (22.15; 29.15) and contrasts with the rod of the avenging deity scourging the sinful (Ezek 20.37; Job 9.34; Job 21.9; Lam 3.1 [contrast Ps 23.4]).[1] The "stripes of the children of men" are most certainly the opposite of the "stripes" (*nega*ʿ) with which God plagued enemies such as the Pharaoh of Egypt (cf. Gen 12.17; Exod 11.1; 1 Kgs 8.37; Ps 91.10). In themselves neither of these punitive strategies imply anything about unconditionality: to the contrary the simple fact of pun-

---

ʾ*anāšîm* stands as a collective parallel to ʾ*āb* in the same way that *bᵉnê* ʾ*ādām* stands as a collective to *bēn*. In any case, the semantic play between the former and latter parts of v. 14 is on the familial metaphor, established in the first part. "I will be a father to him and he a son to me." The punitive dimension is explored in the latter part.

1. Given the ironic twist of many an oracle, it is not inconceivable that the diminished rod of men bears a taste of the Assyrian rod of affliction (cf. Isa 9.3 [4]; 10.5; 10.24; 30.31).

ishment suggests the opposite. The point of the diminutions is limita-
tion of punishment in comparison with what happened to Saul, not its
elimination.

Commentators, especially subsequent to Weinfeld's article on
covenants of grant (1970), usually remark on how the language of v. 14
supports the notion of an unconditional allotment to the Davidides. But
this vocabulary is constrained by the familial metaphor that God
chooses as a contrast to his relationship with Saul. Moreover, the focus
of the verse on sin and punishment suggests that we need be cautious
about reading "unconditionality" in the verse. It is easy to forget, in the
context of all the conditions attached to the Sinai covenant, that 2 Sam
7.14 never explicitly says anything about "unconditionality."
Furthermore, when God says "I will be (*'anî 'ehyeh*) a father to him,"
the verbal form (1st sing. imperfect of *hyh*) adverts to the covenantal
language of Sinai, which God has already used in v. 9 to remind David
of the obligation that is the price of divine presence. "I will be to him a
father and he to me a son" contains another strong echo of the
covenantal language of Sinai, namely, "I will be God to you and you a
people to me" (cf. Exod 6.7; Lev 26.12; Jer 7.23; 11.4; 30.22;
Ezek 36.28; Hos 1.9). Last, but not least, the familial language of v. 14
echoes that of v. 12, the description of David's passing on to his fathers
and being surpassed by his successor. Now Yahweh steps in as the
orphaned Davidide's father and sonship is transferred from David. This
move is another subtle reminder to David that he has no personal role
to play in the new plans that God lays out here.

Verse 15, like v. 14, is a three part affair whose theme, unity, and
parts are marked by a developing series of repetitions. The repetitions
bear variations which harbour much of the implicit rhetorical freight:

wᵉhasdî	*lō'-yāsûr*	*mimmennû*
ka'ᵃšer	*hᵃsirōtî*	*mē'im šā'ûl*
'ᵃšer	*hᵃsirōtî*	*millᵉpāneykā*

Figure 16. Structure in 2 Samuel 7.15

God introduces a contrast to the portrait painted in v. 14 with the key
covenantal term, *hesed*. "My favour" (McCarter's translation) "shall not
turn from him." Putting "favour" as subject of the verb here, God
makes it sound as though "favour" were a divine emanation with a
mind of its own, something naturally inalienable to David's successor.

But compared to what is it so? The grammatical role played by "favour" in the first part is in marked contrast to the two other occurrences of the same verb. Yahweh is subject of both, the first of which has "favour" as object, the second, Saul himself. The noun/relative pronoun at the beginning of each line moves from "favour" as subject of the verb to "the which," i.e., "favour" as object, to "whom," i.e., Saul as object. The contrast, which grows in intensity from the second to the third parts, both of which stand opposite the first, is between a "favour" that seems native to David's successor and a "favour" that God puts away from Saul whom God ultimately puts away from before David. Opposite one neutrally presented "it shall not turn," stand two "I put away" forms of the verb, the first aimed against Saul's best interest, the second against Saul himself. The epistrophic repetition of the preposition *min* at the end of each line makes the same point ring out. The first line, "from him" is simple and uncompounded: "favour" shall not turn from him. The second is more complex, *mēʿim*, the doubled prepositions suggesting that "favour" was never so native to Saul when God removed it from him. The third also has a compounded preposition, *millepāneykā*, that supports the sharpening of the onslaught against Saul that is the whole point of the third line: the "putting away" is not just "favour" from Saul, it is Saul himself that is put away. So now, in the third line, it is more than "favour" that is put away "from with Saul"; it is Saul so put away "from before you."

Obviously, God is going to great length to assure David that what happened to the house of Saul will not happen to the house of David. The developmental contrast within v. 15 makes that point most strongly. But there is another implicit point that is best seen in the combination of vv. 14 and 15. Each has a three part structure and the point is made obvious by setting the two verses, arranged by their three part structure, side by side:

V. 14	V. 15
I will be a father to him and he a son to me.	And my favour will not turn from him,
Which, when he goes astray, I will correct	which (favour) I put away from with Saul,
with the rod of men, the stripes of the sons of men.	whom I put away from before you

Both verses begin with promising portrayals of how things will be with David's successor: father and son with the former's favour having its own self-directed proclivity to the successor. The contrast begins in the second part of each verse. When David's successor goes astray he is corrected, in much the same manner that God had historically corrected Israel rather than rejecting it in its long history of covenantal defections. Of course, as the commentaries have noted, the correction promised here is even lighter, in keeping with the familial metaphor. It seems, as God intends, that the Davidides will have it easier than any before. Saul was different. When he went astray Yahweh removed his favour forthwith (1 Sam 15).[1] First "favour," then Saul himself were summarily put away. And where there will be the "rod and stripes of man," Saul was himself put away from before David. Why? Specifically for transgression against the law of the "ban" (*ḥerem*) by the pitfall of avarice (1 Sam 15.9). Certainly Saul's fate is not without precedent (cf. Josh 7 and the sin of Achan). But God has already shown himself willing to relax that same law more than once (cf. Eslinger 1989:25–54, 78–80; Judg 2.23). More than transgressor, Saul is victim. He was in the right place at the wrong time. He was the king that Israel imposed on Yahweh and thus the king that Yahweh eliminates at first opportunity. What then, is God saying to David? Explicitly, that the house of David has a certain and positive future quite unlike that of the house of Saul. The point of reference back to the house of Saul may, once again, betray Yahweh's reading of David's motive for building a temple: to try and secure his house against anything like the fate of the house of Saul.

Implicitly, however, there is quite another, less promising side to this comparison. David's successor is not off the hook, not able to do as he pleases without regard to divine standards of behaviour. Quite the

---

1. The incident in 1 Samuel 15 is the first time that Saul strays from God's directive. The events of 1 Samuel 13 are not accounted by God as defections, only by Samuel. But God makes no allowance, leaves no room for making amends (1 Sam 15.10–11). Why? Because the kingship of Saul is something imposed on the divinity by the people's request. Certainly God does revise the quality of Saul's monarchy, establishing him within the theocracy as *nāgîd*. But Saul remains a king on the throne because of Israel's initiative, not God's. Yahweh therefore takes the first opportunity to remove Saul and establish a king after his own heart (1 Sam 15.11; 16.1, 7, 12). Saul's fate is extraordinary in the light of the performance of the nation as a whole and how God deals with it. By analogy, Israel's history would have ended in Exodus 16 or earlier.

contrary: Yahweh focuses the future of the house on punishment for its misdeeds.[1] He might have talked about expanding borders or heaps of gold (cf. 1 Kgs 3.12–13), but he chooses to remind that sin bears its consequence. The comparative silver lining to this clouded future is that there will be no such fate as met the unfortunate Saul. Though God has been moved to allow a temple by David's own effrontery, not his own sense of timing, the successor who will build this temple will not find himself in the same position as Saul, the compromise king. But the contrast implicitly allows anything up to but not including the un-forgiving removal of Saul. The full measure of obligation remains.[2] The familial metaphor of v. 14, combined with that verse's suggestions about limited punishments take their contextual cue, their comparative point of reference, from the summary judgement executed against the house of Saul. The "rod of men and stripes of the sons of men" are more bait to lure David's acquiescence, but they must be interpreted against the parallel part in v. 15: "[Saul], whom I put away from before you." Of course David may be expected, as in fact he does, to miss the subtle implications of the parallel that God draws between this scenario and that which brought Saul to the throne.

Only now (v. 16), after an extensive digression into the future of the house and David's successor, does Yahweh come back to the topic with which he began in v. 11b: "Yahweh declares to you that Yahweh will

---

1. It is difficult to find in such a vision of the future a "blank check of unlimited validity" (so Tsevat 1964:73). Cf. Campbell (1986:74), who senses what a two-edged sword the rod of men might be (but he attributes that rhetorical purpose to "prophetic redactors" rather than to Yahweh).

2. Reading in the localized context of Yahweh's rhetoric brings me to a much different conclusion than Weinfeld, who reads in the context of A.N.E. covenants of grant: "What is then meant in II Sam. VII, 14 is that when David's descendants sin they will be disciplined like rebellious sons by their father but they will not be alienated" (1970:193). My understanding of the function of genre is guided by studies such as that of Alastair Fowler (1982 ["the major modern study," "Genre," *The New Princeton Encyclopedia of Poetry and Poetics* (ed. A. Preminger *et al.*; Princeton: Princeton University Press, 1993), 456–58]), who suggests that generic codes are always modulated by the rhetorical goals of the immediate circumstance of use. Furthermore, Weinfeld does admit that his reading of Yahweh's promise does not accord with the conventions for treatment of rebellious sons in A.N.E. literature, forcing him to suppose "a special privilege and apparently given for extraordinary loyal service" (p. 193).

make a house for *you*."[1] Having shown in detail how it will be David's successor, not David, and "a house for my name," not "a house for me to live in," Yahweh sums up the great promise of v. 11. Verse 16 is weakly linked to v. 15 by the preposition "before" (*lipnē*). Verse 15 closes with a recollection of Saul put away "from before" David; v. 16a concludes that David's house is secure "before" him forever. This connection reiterates the main contrast of vv. 14–15, that David's house would not end in the manner of Saul's. Much stronger links connect v. 16 with v. 13, making for another large enveloping structure running from vv. 13–16:

> v. 13 *hū' yibneh-bayit lišmī*
> *wekōnantī 'et-kissē' mamlaktô 'ad-'ôlām*
> v. 14 The father/son relationship; limited punishment
> v. 15 compared to the treatment of Saul
> v. 16 *wene'man bêtekā ûmamlaktekā 'ad-'ôlām lepāneykā*
> *kis'akā yihyeh nākôn '-ad-'ôlām*

Figure 17. Structure in 2 Samuel 7.13–16

The vocabulary connections between v. 13 and v. 16 are obvious, though there is no evident effort to make any strict pattern of parallelism between the lines. Yahweh's points are clear enough. Having defined exactly what kind of temple the successor will build (for my name), Yahweh can now say "your house will be confirmed"; having stated that it was the throne of the successor's kingdom that would be established (*kwn*), Yahweh can now say "your kingdom will be confirmed … your throne will be established"; and having proclaimed that it was the successor's reign that would go on in perpetuity (*'ad-'ôlām*), Yahweh now takes the liberty to emphasize to David that his house will thus go on before him (*lepāneykā*). There is great emphasis on the security being announced to David; a more subtle emphasis, perhaps, on the fact that these things would be enacted only for David's successor, making David's a stagnant Janus-faced point that looks back to Saul,

---

1. In vv. 11–12 there are two second person pronouns identifying David as recipient of the promises. In v. 12 there are six second person pronouns referring to David in the context of describing the future house, but all of these refer to David's passing on and being succeeded by his own seed. In vv. 12–15 there are ten third person references to the successor, the clear favourite for the position of recipient of the promises.

"put away from before you," and forward to the successor, through whom David could know of a well-established house stretching out before him (*lᵉpāneykā*).

In this reading of Yahweh's speech I have been concerned to draw out the undertones and subtle implications. These things are in the speech but they have often been overlooked as readers, much in the manner of David himself, concentrate on those promissory aspects of the speech that suggest that Yahweh is giving away something unprecedented. That, of course, is Yahweh's rhetorical guise. Only a painstaking analysis, with careful attention to the literary allusiveness of the speech, reveals the sleight of hand. On the topic of subtlety, it is worthwhile to compare Yahweh's speech with David's speeches. Yahweh is dictatorial where David is conciliatory. As God and benefactor, he is in a position to make demands where David can only make requests. Yahweh's rhetoric, while it does take some interesting turnabouts, has a less seductive quality than that of David, who must, he thinks, lure the deity into an obligation that he might not make without alluring demonstrations.

We come back to an earlier question: if Yahweh refuses the temple and really gives away nothing new to David here, why take such a circuitous route? Why not just say no to the temple, no to David, and omit all of the supposed face-lifting on covenantal accountability? For Yahweh to have done so would be, to say the least, trivial. But as effective? The fact that he did not do so, combined with the wide-ranging topics that he introduces, suggests that he wanted to do and in fact does more. His speech encompasses the temple, recasting it according to divine standards, and the Davidic house, also carefully positioned within the existing framework of divine standards for the monarchy. As with the earlier request for a king, the deity seizes David's request for a temple as an opportunity to remake something threatening to the theocracy into something that can be incorporated within it. The "king like all the nations" becomes the deity's "designate" (*nāgîd*) (cf. 1 Sam 8.5 → 1 Sam 16) and the temple for God's abode, the temple for God's name (cf. 2 Sam 7.5 → 2 Sam 7.13).

Chapter 3

DAVID'S RESPONSE (2 SAM 7.18–29)

VERSE 17 (INTERLUDE)

In v. 17 the narratorial voice intrudes briefly again. The interlude intimates a silence, reminding the reader of narratorial reticence and the guise a neutral, dispassionate telling. What is represented about this "conversation" between Yahweh and David needs no overt commentary: its importance is best deduced from the unfolding repartee. It is the relationship between king and God, in process of definition through this verbal sparring match, that is important. Of course the narrator/author has built a perspectival interpretation into what is reported. But the strategy of reportage here is to let the conversants play out, through their interaction, what is at issue and how it is resolved. If the narrative can be said to be "about" something, it is about the power struggle between the thrones of heaven and earth.

The content of the narratorial intrusion is slim and seems, at first glance, tediously repetitious. More or less the same thing gets said three different ways—that Nathan told all to David:

> $k^e k\bar{o}l$ $hadd^e b\bar{a}r\hat{i}m\ h\bar{a}^{}\hat{e}lleh$
> $\hat{u}k^e k\bar{o}l$ $hah izz\bar{a}y\hat{o}n\ hazzeh$
> $k\bar{e}n$ $dibber\ n\bar{a}t\bar{a}n\ ^{}el-d\bar{a}wid$

Figure 18. Repetition in 2 Sam 7.17

But the repetition is not without significance. From the narratorial emphasis, readers know that David responds to the same thing that we have heard in the divine speech, not to a revision in which the prophet may have sweetened or soured the message. If David agrees to Yahweh's proposal, as indeed he does, he will be bound by all its implications, no matter how indisposed David is to hear them at this particular, emotion-ridden moment.

David structures his second piece using a series of enveloping parallels. The centre of the structure stands in the parallels between v. 25 and v. 26. In this envelope (cf. W.G.E. Watson 1984:282–87) the lines of vv. 18–24 run parallel, though not in a rigid one-to-one manner, to those of vv. 25–29. This semo-structural symmetry supports David's fundamental proposition: what God has promised to do for David mirrors what God had already done in the foundational event, the exodus. It is just as significant, just as honourable. The structure is aimed at binding two constitutive events. It proposes equal benefit for God and man from each divine benefaction. Of course Israel and David do profit from the divine action, but God has no less a reward in the great glorification that flows from his own acts. Throughout the structure, David adapts his argument for the security of his throne to terms of reference and assumptions to which Yahweh has just demonstrated affiliation.[1] David wants God's guarantee for his dynasty so he tries, rhetorically, to glue together an uncertain support for his interests with God's unwavering commitment to the exodus/Sinai covenant. According to C. Perelman's analysis of argumentation (1982:81, cf. p. 21), such a strategy is exactly what is required when a speaker wishes to transfer adherence from audience-accepted premises to the speaker's innovative conclusion: "As soon as elements of reality are associated with each other in a recognized liaison, it is possible to use this liaison as the basis for an argumentation which allows us to pass from what is accepted to what we wish to have accepted."

THE STRUCTURE OF DAVID'S REJOINDER

A 18 Then went king David in, and sat before the LORD, and he said, Who am I, O Lord GOD? and what is my house, that thou hast brought me hitherto?

B 19 And this was yet a small thing in thy sight, O Lord GOD; but thou hast spoken also of thy servant's house for a great while to come. May that be the law for the people [Fokkelman's trans.], O Lord GOD?

C 20 And what can David say more unto thee? for thou, Lord GOD, knowest thy servant.

C 21 For thy word's sake, and according to thine own heart, hast thou done all these great things, to make thy servant know them.

C 22 Wherefore thou art great, O LORD God: for there is none like thee, neither is there any God beside thee, according to all that we have heard with our ears.

1. When God chose to use the exodus and conquest events as an argument by example against David's proposition, he became committed to those terms (cf. Perelman, 1969:353). David now plays on another aspect of that admitted reliance on such terms of reference.

D	23	And what one nation in the earth is like thy people, even like Israel, whom God went to redeem for a people to himself, and to make him a name, and to do for you great things and terrible, for thy land, before thy people, which thou redeemedst to thee from Egypt, from the nations and their gods?
E	24	For thou hast confirmed (*kwn*; cf. vv. 13, 16, 26[1]) to thyself thy people Israel to be a people unto thee for ever: and thou, LORD, art become their God.
E'	25	And now, O LORD God, the word that thou hast spoken concerning thy servant, and concerning his house, establish it for ever, and do as thou hast said.
D'	26	And let thy name be magnified for ever, saying, The LORD of hosts is the God over Israel: and let the house of thy servant David be established before thee.
C'	27	For thou, O LORD of hosts, God of Israel, hast revealed to thy servant, saying, I will build thee an house: therefore hath thy servant found in his heart to pray this prayer unto thee.
B'	28	And now, O Lord GOD, thou art that God, and thy words be true, and thou hast promised this goodness unto thy servant:
A'	29	Therefore now let it please thee to bless the house of thy servant, that it may continue for ever before thee: for thou, O Lord GOD, hast spoken it: and with thy blessing let the house of thy servant be blessed for ever.

Figure 19. Structure of 2 Sam 7.18–29

VERSE 18

David's first move, aimed at Yahweh's apparent displeasure at his effrontery (v. 8) is to smooth the deity's ruffled feathers. The phrasing, "who am I, O Lord God, and what is my father's house," recalls Moses' abnegation (Exod 3.18) and David's own (1 Sam 18.18). Answering the belittling tone of Yahweh's reminders (vv. 5, 8), David abases himself and his vaunted "house" (of cedar)[2] which he had dared

---

1. Fokkelman (1990:247) notes the oddity of saying that God "*kwn*" Israel as people rather than the more familiar "*hyh*." But he rejects the connection with the use of the verb in the preceding context.

2. No doubt David, abasing himself, refers to his patrimony, but the play and the parallel with the royal house of cedar that he mentions in v. 2 is explicit and semantically harmonic with the obvious reference to familial stature.

to compare favourably with the sacred tent (v. 2). The loftiness of man is indeed become low here (cf. Isa 2.17), so it seems (cf. Fokkelman, 1990:236). But David is not one to take anything lying down (note his deathbed bloodthirst in 1 Kgs 2). By the end of his response he reverses his self-depreciating, back-tracking thanks for what God has done for him. In place of wonderment at what God has done for him ($h^ab\bar{\imath}^{\prime}\bar{o}tan\hat{\imath}$ ^cad-$h^al\bar{o}m$), David offers no less than four directives to God to do as he has said ($h\bar{a}q\bar{e}m$ ... $wa^ca\acute{s}\bar{e}h$ [v. 25]; $h\bar{o}^{\prime}\bar{e}l$ ... $\hat{u}b\bar{a}r\bar{e}k$ [v. 29]). The contrast between David's beginning and his end is highlighted by the parallelism and the rhyme between his initial wonderment and concluding demands:

$\hat{u}m\hat{\imath}$ $b\bar{e}t\hat{\imath}\ k\hat{\imath}\ h^ab\hat{\imath}^{\prime}\bar{o}tan\hat{\imath}$ ^cad-$h^al\bar{o}m$

$\hat{u}b\bar{a}r\bar{e}k$ $^{\prime}et$- $b\bar{e}t\ ^cabd^ek\bar{a}\ lihy\bar{o}t$ $l^c\bar{o}l\bar{a}m$

Figure 20. Parallels between 2 Sam 7.18 and 29

The relationship between the beginning and end in David's response is part of an overall pattern in his speech that echoes the stages in Yahweh's. Yahweh began by putting a full stop to any silliness about David, of all people, building a temple for God (see Figure 4, p. 27); then he reminded David of his own small place in the covenantal scheme of obligation (see Figure 5, p. 28); and finally he expanded a vision of a new benefaction for the house of David (vv. 12–16). David's speech mirrors all but the first segment (vv. 5–7) of Yahweh's speech, for that proposal is now an embarrassing lost cause. Unlike Yahweh, whose reasons for dwelling on David's humble beginning are clear, David has no impelling reason to do more than formally recognize that direction in Yahweh's speech. The "who am I ..." rhetorical question in v. 18 is all that David needs or wants to offer by way of abnegation. From v. 19 onward his deprecations metamorphose and a new version of divine obligation towards the royal worm crawls out of the cocoon of humiliation.

James Nohrnberg (1991:93) treats David's humble question too naively. He says that David's question is not like that of Shakespeare's Richard II, a narcissistic ego contemplating its own demise. Rather, "The question asks who David is politically, what significant power or position he will enjoy." Nohrnberg misses the possibility that the question is feigned humility voiced with the serious intention of gulling God.

VERSE 19

David's first word in v. 19 continues in what first seems the same vein. "This was but a trifle in your eyes, my lord Yahweh ..." The reader expects that David continues by speaking about something from his past that was unworthy of Yahweh's attention.[1] Instead, it is the very content of Yahweh's promises that David characterizes with the words 'this was but a trifle' (*wattiqtan 'ôd*)! David might be hinting at the possibility that he knows there are not many real gains in the promises, but he couches the valuation as Yahweh's, "[small] in your eyes." The tag turns cheek to compliment: 'how great thou art.' Still, David does seem more than a little impressed with what God has said and works hard to secure it for himself. The surprising switch in the target of his diminutions makes room to extol the awesome abilities of Yahweh—the surface rhetorical strategy that dominates most of vv. 19–26—and to downplay, nonchalantly, the extent of the promise in David's eyes and his excitement about it.

The word "this" (*zô't*) plays a key role, both here (two times in v. 19) and in the mirroring parallels near the end of David's speech in v. 28.[2] What exactly does David refer to by this vague demonstrative pronoun? What to make of the difficult clause in which the second

---

1. On the technique of creating expectation and then surprising it, see Stanley Fish's study, *Surprised by Sin. The Reader in Paradise Lost* (1967). A.A. Anderson (1989:126) finds a suggestion of exilic orientation in the appeal to Yahweh to fulfill his word. "Our impression is that the fervent appeals to Yahweh to fulfill his promises to David may imply that the actual circumstances of the author have called in question, in some way or other, this very fulfillment. Consequently, the exilic period would provide a good historical setting for this prayer." Perhaps, and the exilic period comes naturally to mind when one tries to imagine a period of duress for the nation. But what is wrong with the duress that David feels both having his dream of a temple smashed and almost in the same breath a vision of security, beyond his wildest hope, for that self-same structure? If there is an intra-textual logic that "explains" a frame of mind represented in the text, how does one decide whether or not one also needs an extra-textual logic to explain it?

2. In all of David's speech it is only in these two verses that the word *zô't* is made to bear such weight. Elsewhere in the speech it is found only in v. 27, where it modifies the word "prayer."

zō't of v. 19 is found?[1] There is some help within the parallel structure of the verse itself:

a *wattiqtan ʿōd zō't bᵉʿēneykā ʾadōnāy yhwh*
b *wattᵉdabbēr gam ʾel-bēt-ʿabdᵉkā lᵉmērāḥōq*
c *wᵉzō't tōrat hāʾādām ʾadōnāy yhwh*

Figure 21. Repetition in 2 Sam 7.19

The first *zō't* obviously refers back, as the demonstrative usually does, to some undefined thing that God has said and/or done; the reach of the phrase is extended in "b," in which *lᵉmērāḥōq* is commonly read, in context, as having future reference.[2] David's use of this temporal expression includes both the lengthy history that Yahweh has traced and also stretches the expression to adduce an equally lengthy future. He succeeds, as recorded readings attest, in turning *lᵉmērāḥōq* from its conventional past reference by contextualizing it so that its temporal reference can be read primarily as future. What is gained? The implication, intimated here and later to be pounded home, is that what has been for eons past shall be; benefactions past shall be extended, likewise, into the far distant future. The first *zō't*, therefore, vaguely refers to what Yahweh has promised and its influence stretches from past performance to future continuation.

The second *zō't* parallels the first (and also the subsequent occurrence in v. 28), stressing the durative emphasis of the first by proposing a societal pervasion of "this" about which Yahweh has spoken and David now speaks. Fokkelman translates the phrase, "May that (*zō't*) be the law for the people," an expression of David's

---

1. S.R. Driver's assessment of conjectural emendations of v. 19 remains valid: "no satisfactory emendations of the passage have been proposed" (1913:277; cf., before Driver, H.P. Smith 1899:302; after Driver, P.K. McCarter 1984:233).

2. Cf., e.g. P. Dhorme (1910:330), "pour un lointain avenir." Of six related occurrences (2 Sam 7.19; 2 Kg 19.25; Isa 37.26; Job 36.3; 39.29; Ezra 3.13; 1 Chron 17.17; 2 Chron 26.15) all seem comprehensible as referring either to a spacious expanse or a long time ago—not a long time to come. Only the context in 2 Sam 7 (cf. 1 Chron 17.17) suggests future reference.

hope that what God has promised might be written in stone.[1] What God has spoken David characterizes as decree, as can be seen from the parallel with v. 28:

B 7:19   a   *wattiqtan ʿŏd zōʾt beʿêneykā ʾadōnāy yhwh*
         b   *watteᵈabbēr gam ʾel-bêt-ʿabdᵉkā leᵐērāḥôq*
         c   *weᶻōʾt tôrat hāʾādām ʾadōnāy yhwh*

Bʹ 7:28 a   *weᶜattā ʾadōnāy yhwh*
         b   *ʾattâ-hûʾ hāʾᵉlōhîm*
             ûdᵉbāreykā yihyû ʾᵉmet
         c   *watteᵈabbēr ʾel-ʿabdᵉkā ʾet-haṭṭôbâ hazzōʾt*

Figure 22. Parallels between 2 Sam 7.19 and 28

There is a pattern to David's words, established in 7.19 and then repeated in v. 28:

19 -glorification of "my lord Yhwh"; "this" was nothing
   -allusion to the content of the divine promise; key: for a long while
   -may "this" be the law of man, my lord Yhwh
28 -And now, my lord Yhwh
   -may your divine words be true
   -i.e., all "this" good that you have spoken [to me]

Viewed from another angle, the parallel is as follows:

19 -"this" was a trifle in your eyes, my lord Yhwh
   - you have spoken, also, to the house of your servant from afar—
     may this be the torah of man, lord Yhwh
28 -and now, lord Yhwh
   -you must honour your divine word, you have spoken to your
     servant all "this" good

Seen from the second angle, there is second pattern that confirms Fokkelman's reading, "May that (*zōʾt*) be the law for the people." The parallel in v. 28 is "you should [by nature] honour your divine word." In both places David wants an iron-clad contract. But it is the first way of viewing the parallelism that most illuminates the awkward *zōʾt* of v. 19. The structural analogy is as straightforward as the

---

1. Cf. Fokkelman 1990:240, "The little opening word "this" refers back to God's speaking on the distant future. This is so powerful and normative (*tōrā*) that the speaker ... speaks of man in general ...."

rhetorical point of each verse. Structural and rhetorical purposes are identical: to take the divine origin of what God has said as, in itself, guarantee of the longevity and irrevocability of what God, as "eternal being without self-contradiction,"[1] has said. Even Yahweh himself should not be able to countermand what he, as "The God-who-cannot-lie" (*ʾattā-hûʾ hāʾelōhîm ûdebāreykā yihyû ʾemet*), has spoken.

VERSES 20–22

Beginning with part "C" (vv. 20–22), David works out a revisionist version of the heavy Sinaitic covenantalism that Yahweh preached (vv. 8–11, see Figure 5, p. 28). Yahweh's review of covenantal history was intended to reawaken David's sense of obligation. So now David acknowledges the divine will and pays homage to his benefactor. David's rhetorical ploy throughout vv. 20–22 (C) and the counterpoised v. 27 (C') is to play on God's personal credibility and honour.[2] David's posture is extreme self-abasement: he claims nothing on his own merit. He addresses Yahweh's unyielding aversion to any hint of human pride (cf. Gen 11; Ezek 17.24) by effacing all traces of the effrontery in his presumption to build a house for God. Even his own generic categorization of his calculated rhetorical response as a "prayer" (v. 27) presents an abject face, however false some might find it, to the lordly deity.

1. Cf. Saadya Gaon's refutation of changeability within divinity, "If someone imagines that these attributes imply a diversity within God, i.e. some difference between the various attributes, I will show him his mistake by pointing out the real truth of the matter, viz. that diversity and change can take place in bodies and their accidents only, but the Creator of all bodies and accidents is above diversity and change" (1956:83).

2. In Aristotle's categories, David's strategy, here and throughout his second speech, is to use "internal" argument (not dependent on external witnesses or documentation) that proposes a future state that depends solely on the credibility of Yahweh (ethos) and on cultivating divine favour by reminding God of the positive consequences for divine reputation (pathos). See *Rhetoric* 1355b,38; 1356a,15; Kennedy (1984:15–19). This is a modification of the normal role of reputability, in which it is the reputation of the speaker on which an argument is made to rest. Having taken the necessary course of abasing himself, groveling some would say, David chooses the most upright character on which to found the reliability of what he proposes.

Lexical and syntactic links between vv. 20–22 and v. 27 are limited to the parallel expressions "to speak to you" (*lᵉdabbēr 'ēleykā* (v. 20) and "to pray to you" (*lᵉhitpallēl 'ēleykā*) (v. 27) and to the duplicate references to hearing: "as we have heard with our ears" (v. 22) and "you have opened the ear of your servant" (v. 27). A stronger connection comes in the form of David's doubled excuse for daring to speak at all:

> And what more can David yet add ...
> ... thus your servant fount it in his heart to pray to you this prayer

Between the two excuses—the sheer bulk of the response puts the lie to the sincerity of v. 20—lies the core of David's response, from which one can abstract the following argument:

C   A revelation leads to speechlessness followed by praise for the incomparable deity (vv. 20–22)

D   Historical review of how God's acts in history have made His name (v. 23)

E   Sinaitic covenantal formula: Israel has become his people *'ad-'ôlām* and he their God (v. 24)

E'   In like manner, Yahweh is called on to establish (*hāqēm*) his words about David *'ad-'ôlām* (v. 25)

D'   Yahweh's name will be magnified *'ad-'ôlām* when it is proclaimed that he is God over Israel and when the house of David is established before him (v. 26).

C'   The great revelation has led the speechless David to pray this prayer (v. 27).

Figure 23. David's Argument in 2 Sam 7.20–27

David's persuasive tack is straightforward, set in a covenantal, "Deuteronomistic" register.[1] There are two sides to this covenantal

---

1. McCarter (1984:237, 240), citing many others who have shared his perception of "Deuteronomisticisms" in vv. 22–26, finds here a Deuteronomistic expansion. That makes the section (v. 22b–26) late and not needing consideration in any attempt to understand David's supposed historical answer to Yahweh. Aside from the way it short-circuits the interpretive process, such typological labeling disallows the rhetorical possibility that a character might use the linguistic register creatively. Certainly David's effort to turn such "official ideology" to his own advantage is far more creative than the supposed plodding Dtr, who can only phrase his thoughts in the same tiresome idiom. Surely the assumption that a linguistic register—first a socio-linguistic concept (cf. D. Crystal 1987:52, 429) and only secondarily historical—is strictly confined to a single narrative voice or a supposed socio-ideological group/period in ancient

coin: Yahweh emphasizes one, David its opposite. Of course David is in no position to make bold demands so he smothers his points in syrup. In God's hands, the covenantal themes of the exodus were played to emphasize obligation and obedience—the natural and just consequence of what God had done for Israel and, more recently, for David too. David takes those same themes, fundamentally the exodus and the personal protection of David on his way to the throne, and extracts from them a certain future in which the very divinity of Yahweh stands surety for David's dynastic future.[1] A bold reversal: how does he try to get away with it?

David's basic argument is analogical: the gains made by God in the exodus will be augmented in the similar actions toward the house of David (cf. Perelman 1982:114–25). To appreciate the rhetorical design in David's analogy, we must follow its unfolding sequential path. The overarching chiastic structure, lifeless when pinned out in a diagram on a page, can only be appreciated as rhetoric step-by-step, especially as each corresponding element in the second half (vv. 25–29) rings out evocatively against the corresponding segment from the first half (vv. 18–24). Of the three broad categories of rhetoric established by Aristotle, David's overall strategy is epideictic: he needs to strengthen the expressed commitment that he hears in Yahweh's speech (see Kennedy 1984:19–20; Aristotle, *Rhetoric*, 1358*b*,5). Praise for what Yahweh has done is a way of convincing Yahweh to do more of the same, at least more of the same as David construes the parallel between past and future acts of covenantal benefaction.

The first step in David's plan includes vv. 18–22 ("A–C" in the chiastic structure). He mitigates the effrontery of his temple building

---

Israel's literary history needs more defending. The definitive study (Weinfeld 1972) provides a typology and glossary that, themselves, rest on a historical assumption. (The section on the scribes (pp. 158–71) is too dependent on the Dtr narrative itself to stand as a stable historical description of the Dtr's historical milieu.) Limited reflection on the rhetorical possibilities of "Dtr-speak" in the Dtr narratives may be found in Eslinger (1989:123–25, 164–65).

1. The redactional method cannot address such complicated rhetorical strategy. Veijola, for example, says that because vv. 22–24 focus on covenantal history, and not the matter of dynasty that is David's pressing concern, they are secondary contributions of a later redactor (1975:74).

bid by groveling for Yahweh: he "sits before" (*wayēšeb lipnê*) Yahweh,[1]
abases himself and his lineage ("who am I ... what is my house" [v.
18]), constantly refers to himself as "your servant" (vv. 19, 20, 21,
25, 26, 27, 28, 29 [2 times]), uses doubled honorifics when addressing
the deity ("my lord Yahweh" [vv. 18, 19 [2 times], 20, 22, 25, 26, 27,
28, 29]), magnifies Yahweh's grace ("you have brought me ..." [v.
18], "it was a trifle in your eyes" [v. 19]), and exalts Yahweh as one
without equal (vv. 22, 23, 26). Though a bit thick, the effusion ought
to lay to rest any worry that God might have had about David
publicly stepping out of line. Of course the rhetoric does nothing to
allay concerns that a reader might entertain about David's true
attitude. More important, other than the fact that ch. 7 ends with
David's response and life carries on normally for David and Yahweh
thereafter (e.g. 8.6; cf. 5.23–25), we have no indication that God
swallows any or all of what David tries to feed him. Whatever the
reception, inside or outside the story world, there is no doubt about

1. That David should "sit" rather than prostrate himself before Yahweh has
raised some eyebrows among commentators (for discussion and rejection of any
impropriety see H.P. Smith 1899:302; E. Dhorme 1910:330). McCarter
(1984:236), following Keil's earlier suggestion (1982:349–50) that such a penitent
posture is not otherwise attested in the Bible, suggests that the verb portrays a
lingering, earnest David. Given the overall shape and attitude expressed in
David's response, however, I am inclined to believe that David's posture is so
described as a subtle supporting hint of his real attitude. He is not prostrate
before Yahweh because he really has no intention to submit absolutely. The
collocation of the verb " to sit" with a royal figure confirms this reading. When
last we saw David sitting in 2 Sam 7, it was "in his house" (cf. v. 1). David, as a
character, is well aware of the special significance his "sitting" has (cf. v. 2). And
hereafter, whenever a royal figure "sits" it is *always* on the throne (e.g., 1 Kgs
1.13, 17, 20, 24, 27, 30, 35, 48; 2.12, 19; 3.6; 8.20, 25; 16.11; 22.10; 2 Kgs 10.30;
11.19; 13.13; 15.12). The associations of a king's "sitting" are particularly clear in
the cluster of occurrences of this idiom in the first three chapters of 1 Kings,
where the succession to the throne is at issue. The fact that Israel's kings never
otherwise sit anywhere other than on their throne (or in the royal house, the
virtual synonym in 2 Sam 7.1) suggests that the usage in v. 18 is not innocent
(cf. Ivan Engnell, *The Call of Isaiah* (1949:16), "As to v. 1 [Isa 6.1] it is worthy of
note that שׁב is a technical term for the sitting on the throne cf., e.g., the use of
the participle as an equivalent of "king" in Am. 1:5, 1:8 etc."; also Othmar Keel
[1977:59 n. 59]). The narrator plants the stock verb here as a preliminary clue to
the oddity of David's pious mis-demeanour. It is as king that David stations
himself before Yahweh here.

David's tactic. He will seek to win Yahweh through praise and submission.

David tightens his grip on what he believes are Yahweh's covenantal heart strings with his talk about reciprocal "knowing" (yd^c):[1]

you know your servant (v. 20)	*we'attâ yādaʿtā ʾet-ʿabdekā*
you have done all these great things (v. 21)	*ʿāśîtā ʾēt kol-haggedûlâ hazzōʾt*
to make your servant know them (v. 21)	*lehôdîaʿ ʾet-ʿabdekā*

Figure 24. The Verb *yd^c* in 2 Sam 7.20–21

According to David, the promises that Yahweh has made constitute, just as surely as Sinai for Israel, the basis of the special covenantal relationship that he, King David ("your servant"), has with Yahweh. The way that David lays out this reciprocal matrix is a microcosm of his overall rhetorical strategy. While praising God for the great things he has done he inevitably mentions the positive consequences for covenantal relations between God and his chosen one. David, of course, is careful to point out that he is not alone in benefiting from what God has and will do. He comes to such conclusions already within vv. 21–22.

First David makes it clear that he sees no outside compulsion that would have constrained Yahweh to make such overtures: "for the sake of your word, according to your heart" (v. 21). Given that God was first mover in this business, he should have no reason to back out after hearing David's version of what he has promised to do. Whatever David might make of it, he wants God to accept (in the momentary blindness of swelling pride of accomplishment?) responsibility for carrying forward what David describes as his initiative.

Consequent to the great thing (*kol-haggedûlâ hazzōʾt*, v. 21) that Yahweh has done—fait accompli (*ʿāśîtā*, v. 21)—Yahweh has himself become great (*ʿal-kēn gādaltā*). So great, in fact, that he is now without equal, a reputation that David, among others, have heard voiced about. Nowhere in this preliminary description of the benefit of

---

1. On the relational or covenantal usage of *yd^c* see G.J. Botterweck (1986:468–70).

God's action is there anything in it for David explicitly: all benefit accrues to God. And what benefit! David picks up on the primary purpose of the exodus event: increasing knowledge of Yahweh through the broadcasting of his great reputation. Only here, it is God himself, not just his reputation, that is enlarged. Having been so bold as to suggest the personal accrual, David tempers his impertinence by alluding to the model of the exodus: "according to all that we have heard with our ears" (v. 22). What one hears with one's ears is the reputation of God, won in the business of mighty acts on behalf of his people. In all of this it is the exodus and all of its associate meaning that David draws into play to lure God. Turnabout being fair play, David does no more here than God did in vv. 8–11, where he used exodus imagery to incorporate David within the fold of those obligated by the exodus event. But "C" (vv. 20–22) is only a prelude to David's rhetorical variations on the exodus theme. "D" (v. 23) moves much more explicitly into the arena of exodus theology and its consequences.

VERSE 23

Though the text of v. 23 is difficult on account of the interchange between singular and plural implied subjects, the sense can be perceived by following the outline of a chiastic structure briefly traced by Fokkelman (1990:244–45).[1]

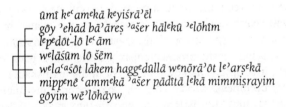

Figure 25. Structure of 2 Sam 7.23

The rhetorical question about Israel's God-given distinctiveness is a follow-up to the incomparability of Yahweh in v. 22, a follow-up that

---

1. The favoured option among text critics depends on A. Geiger's discussion of the text (1857; 2nd ed., 1928:288–89). J. Wellhausen (1871:173), for example, suggests that the reading of LXX be adopted—*gōy 'aḥēr* rather than *gōy 'eḥad*—and then supplemented by correcting plurals to singulars.

details the beneficent side effect of God's own magnificence (Fokkelman 1990:244). First the divine benefit; then the human side-effect. God is great for what he does; Israel gets swept along, show-ered by good fortune in the tail of God's meteoric brightness.

David opens his peroration on Israel's unique status with a point-edly generic description. Israel is simply one of the nations, "*gôy*," and Yahweh is one of the "gods." The plural, *hālᵉkû*, of which "the gods" are subject is therefore part of David's intention. *ʾᵉlōhîm* refers here to that god amongst gods who distinguishes himself, and thus his people, by ransoming Israel as his peculiar possession amongst the nations (cf. Exod 19.5; Deut 4.7, 34; 14.2; 26.18). Prior to that act both god and nation are indistinguishable from the rest. *Both* become distinguished through the divine acts that follow. There is an obvious vector of development in v. 23: from pre-exodus, generic de-scription, to dispassionate description of the exodus purpose and consequences for the deity (third person pronouns describe the deity to the deity), to involved, confessional description of the same exodus event (cf. Fokkelman 1990:245), but focusing on the resulting possession, Israel by God (second person pronouns addressing the deity directly), and finally returning to a transformed generic de-scription of God and Israel, post-exodus event. The concluding ellip-tic, resumptive phrase, "nation(s)[1] and its God" returns to rehearse the same generic categories as the initial "one nation in the land where gods went ...," but with a difference: there is now a possessive connection between the once unrelated nation and its god. The events that have brought about this association are related in the in-tervening structure describing God's great acts of redemption.

The first stages in the process remain generic: a god goes to claim, for himself, a people. Thereby, one of the indistinguishable nations (*gôy ʾeḥād*) becomes a people (*lᵉʿām*). The second consequence and benefit of this first step is that the god thereby makes a name for himself. Israel is given the status of being a "people" and a god, which

---

1. The plural, *gôyim*, refers to Israel alone in Gen 17.4–6, 16 [Abraham] and in Gen 35.11 [Jacob]. Nevertheless, the plural reference stands out in 2 Sam 7.23: it may be a conscious effort to suggest the fulfillment of the patriarchal promises through the divine act in the exodus. The symmetry that bifurcates v. 23 stands against readings that find in this plural "nations" a reference to nations other than Israel (against, e.g., Wellhausen 1871:173).

is to say Yahweh, wins a reputation.[1] Each needs the other in this process of blessing: David's rehearsal of covenant history, unlike Yahweh's previous rendition, points out the symbiotic nature of the process, though he is at pains to underline the positive consequences for the divinity (no less than five pronominal references describe benefits for God). The generic purview of the first half evaporates in the second. Fokkelman suggests that David breaks forth in a paean to his Lord (1990:245). But the second person address may betray less a bursting heart than a calculated rhetoric to shade the relationship that occurred when the "god" ransomed a "nation" "for a people": in the process, "he" becomes "you" and a bond of obligation has congealed. Of course David does not deny the benefaction that has occurred. He celebrates it because from that point on Israel (and David) can call on the god as "you" and because that god has, in the process, won himself a name. The parallelism in the infinitive purpose clauses ($l^ep^edōt-lō$ // $w^elāśūm\ lō$ // $w^ela^ca\dot{s}ōt\ lākem$) highlights the pairing of benefactions but proposes a reflexive reward for the deity that is twofold to Israel's[2] single benefaction.

1. In this, David shows that he is as good as Yahweh in playing on the apparent character weaknesses of his rhetorical partner. Yahweh had promised David reputation (v. 9); David, knowing that widespread reputation is dear to the heart of this deity, responds with the traditional theology that Yahweh has made a praise-worthy name through his exodus adventures.

2. Parallelism and the sense of the verse demand that $lākem$ be emended to $lāhem$, thus reading "to do for them the great (deed)" rather than "to do for you ...." The overarching verse structure, in which this third purpose clause parallels the second as the benefaction to Israel parallels that to God, supports such an emendation. So does the parallelism within this line:

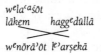

The parallelism between "the great thing" and "wondrous sights" is obvious; the parallelism of the beneficiaries is also apparent when "your land" is understood as a metonym for Israel (cf. Gen 41.57; Waltke, O'Connor 1990:109 [§6.6.b; §34.3.d, # 21, 22]).

Finally, there is the actantial parallel with v. 24 in which Yahweh establishes for himself, once more ($l^ekā$), Israel as a people and he becomes God "for them"

The actual benefaction to Israel is limited to one thing, described two ways: "to do for them the great thing, the awesome [events] for your country." The first word, *hagge͏̣dūllā*, is not much used to describe the exodus deeds (cf. Ps 145.6). It stands out, therefore, as a link back to what David has just mentioned in v. 21: the "great [thing]" that God has done for David. The rhetoric melds the treatment of David with the greatest covenantal benefaction Israel had ever known, the exodus. The combination of the faceless "greatness" with the awesome deeds of the exodus pinpoints revelation as the heart of the benefaction, as does the exodus story itself (cf. Eslinger 1991). At the centre of his historical recitation David has paired the making of the divine reputation with Israel's knowledge of God through those fearsome events—exactly in the manner God envisions himself at the time (cf. Exod 10.1–2).

Winding down from his key pair David returns to reiterate the point about God being the author of this union of people and God. Only now, post climactic, revelatory centre, the relationship is painted in much more personal terms. The revelation was done "on account of *your* people, whom you redeemed *for yourself* from Egypt." David does want to play on God's attachments due to the exodus events—thus the seemingly incidental reference to Egypt, though references to Egypt always make an impact in biblical circles—but more than that he wants to cement God's bond with his people, David included, and thus to pave the way for claims against that historical relationship.

VERSE 24

As a whole, v. 23 (D in the scheme of David's speech) is preparatory to the two central verses: v. 24 (E) and v. 25 (E'). The strategy that controls the sequence and wording of vv. 24–25 is, in terms of rhetorical categories, a modified form of epideictic deduction. David parades the Sinai covenant as something accomplished, though in David's version it is framed in unconventional terms. Then David goes on to characterize the promise that he perceives in Yahweh's speech in the same vein as his modified Sinai covenant. His deduction is that since Sinai was much the same as what God has just promised

(*lāhem*). (For a brief description of actantial analysis in narrative see D. Coste 1989:134–37.)

David, the promises to David can be added on, as an amendment, to the tail of the established, venerable Sinaitic covenant.

Deductive rhetoric, according to Aristotle, is a "proof, or apparent proof, *provided by the words of the speech itself*" (*Rhetoric*, 1356a 3, my emphasis). David's case for an amendment to the Sinaitic covenant depends entirely on the words that he chooses to create an "obvious" parallelism between Sinai and his promises. In "E" (v. 24) he includes formulaic covenantal language, with parallel, pleonastic references to both Israel, "your people, Israel," and God, "you, Yhwh." Using this phrasing he beats the drum of covenantal fidelity. The pattern, 'they, to you, a people; you, to them, a God,' is an atomic formulation of the covenant between God and Israel.[1] It is difficult to think of a stronger way to frame the relationship. David needs this robust, but conventional formulation as a counterweight to the strong modifications he adds. He claims that God "established" (*kwn*) Israel for his people *'ad-'ôlām*. Whether David is to be counted among those who think that the temporal phrase implies an eternity is moot. But the idea of perpetuity is conveyed both by the weaker reading of the temporal phrase and by the verb with which David here blends it. To say that God has "established/constituted" Israel as his people is a much stronger, more vivid and permanent way of describing Israel's status as covenant people (cf. Fokkelman 1990:247). The key point and word here is *kwn*, "establish." With it, David picks up on Yahweh's use of the term in vv. 12–13, where God promises to "establish" (*kwn*) the throne of David's descendent. Now David extends the application of the word so that Sinai becomes David's own pseudonymous prophet, a portent of what God has promised for David's throne. "You "established" for yourself your people Israel as a people for yourself *'ad-'ôlām*." Just as he had promised David a dynasty *'ad-'ôlām* (v. 13), so he is supposed to have promised to "establish" Israel as a people *'ad-'ôlām*. The "indefinite term" adjustment to Sinai brings it into line with the promise to David.

---

1. Cf. Hos 1.9; 2.3, 25. Fokkelman (1990:247 n. 77) provides a full list of scriptural echoes.

VERSE 25

"And now" (*weʿattâ*), with which David begins "Eʹ" (v. 25), signals the turning point in the speech.[1] Everything said thus far is brought to bear on David's own situation. Again, David addresses Yahweh formally: "And now, Yahweh God ...." But a deferential manner can do little to assuage the importunity of a request such as David's: it may, in fact, only make it more obvious by implicit acknowledgment. To this point, everything with the exception of God doing "for them" (i.e., Israel in v. 23) or being God "for them" (v. 24) has been "for him" (i.e., God in v. 23) or 'for/regarding you' (again, referring to God).[2] David continues that emphasis here, "the word that *you* spoke about *your* servant ... as *you* said," but slips in a single pronominal referent that will redound to his own benefit: "the word that you spoke about your servant and about *his* house." The new pronominal direction is bold, but more surreptitious than the verbs by which David directs Yahweh's newly directed concern for his servant's well-being: "The word that you spoke ... *establish* it ʿad-ʿôlām and *do* just as you said [you would]." Where one might expect a plaintive jussive from the petitioning king there are two imperatives. What speechlessness (v. 20) is this?

The parallel between "Eʹ" and "E" reveals what David hopes to gain by his forthrightness:

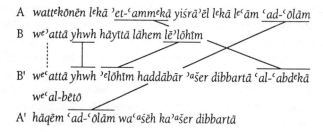

A   *wattᵉkōnēn lᵉkā ʾet-ʿammᵉkā yiśrāʾēl lᵉkā lᵉʿām ʿad-ʿôlām*

B   *weʾattâ yhwh hāyîtā lāhem lēʾlōhîm*

Bʹ *weʿattâ yhwh ʾᵉlōhîm haddābār ʾᵃšer dibbartā ʿal-ʿabdᵉkā*
    weʿal-bētô

Aʹ *hāqēm ʿad-ʿôlām waʿᵃˢēh kaʾᵃšer dibbartā*

Figure 26. Parallels between 2 Sam 7.24 and 25

1. A couple of important parallels to this usage may be found in 1 Sam 12.2 (on which see T. Veijola 1977:92f. and J.R. Vannoy 1978:11 n. 5) and in 1 Kgs 8.26.

2. There are no less than 24 such pronominal references in. vv. 18–24.

The pattern of relationship is an envelope. The conversion of Sinai into a covenant ʿad-ʿōlām obviously paves the way for David to reiterate what Yahweh had said about his house. More than that, it is an effort to show that such an extended period of efficacy is no more than a reiteration of the standard Sinaitic pattern. Furthermore, we can also appreciate why David chose the unusual verb *kwn* to describe the "establishment" of Israel. It is a nice, matching counterpart to the imperative "establish" (*hāqēm*) by which he directs God not to renege on his apparent largesse. Rounding off the parallelism, the two "B" elements begin with rhyming addresses to the deity, *weʾattā yhwh* // *weʿattā yhwh*, both describing acts by which the deity has bound himself to a covenant partner, Israel or David. The claim at the centre of David's speech is that the promises that God has made are fully part of the old Sinaitic pattern, albeit viewed through David's revisionary spectacles. From such perspective, it is more Sinai than the "Davidic" that is shaped in the image of its shadow.

In his matching denouement, from D' (v. 26) to A' (v. 29), David has two aims: to show again how much God has to gain from so blessing David (v. 26) and most of all, through the opportunity afforded by parallel structure, to say yet again what he hopes God will do (vv. 26–29). The denouement advances no new arguments to support the Davidic cause.

VERSE 26

"D'" (v. 26) is explicitly linked to its antecedent ("D", v. 23) by parallel references to the business of divine reputation, magnification of which is consequent to his association with Israel and now with the house of David. In v. 23 God's name was made, fully in accord with the exodus traditions, by doing what he did for Israel in the exodus. Now, following the alignment of the house of David with the Israelite people, it is God's association with the new conglomerate that brings such glory to the name of God (*weyigdal šimkā*). The exact name to be made by this new alliance is the combination, name + epithet, "Yahweh Sebaoth." The enlarged epithet (in fact, in v. 23 no divine title is mentioned at all) is another hint at the greater benefit that redounds from association with the Davidic house. Last but not least to be mentioned, the dynasty ʿad-ʿōlām that God had offered to David, is repaid as a benefit to God. When the house of David endures *'ad-'ōlām* so does the extension of divine reputation: *weyigdal šimkā 'ad-'ōlām*. The unending (*'ad-'ōlām*) spread of divine repute is an interesting twist on David's re-patterning of Sinai/house of David as unending (*'ad-'ōlām*, vv. 24–25). However David understands the phrase *'ad-'ōlām*, he thinks the result equally attractive to Yahweh.

The structure of "D'" reveals how tightly David wants God to conceive of his newly designed covenantal relationship with Israel. The chiastic parallelism between the second and third lines of v. 26, God over Israel // house of David before God, displays the new dyad that promotes the result mentioned in the first line. Henceforth, this is how God's name will be glorified.

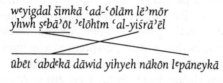

$$w^e yigdal \ šimkā \ 'ad-'ōlām \ lē'mōr$$
$$yhwh \ ṣebā'ōt \ 'elōhîm \ 'al-yiśrā'ēl$$

$$ûbêt \ 'abd^ekā \ dāwid \ yihyeh \ nākōn \ l^epāneykā$$

Figure 27. Structure of 2 Sam 7.26

'May David's house be established (*nākōn*) before you.' Having prepared the way in v. 24 with an exodus event that "established" the people, David groups his house with Israel as just one more of God's establishments. He petitions for no more than what has already been promised him (vv. 12–13) and allotted, in David's version, at Sinai. Most of all in "D'," David strives to cement the association between the house of David and Israel and between both of those entities and the business of divine repute. The rhetoric is epideictic: David seeks a prosperous destiny for his house by drawing God's attention to how much the deity's personal reputation will grow. Favouring the house of David now will do as much as the exodus did for God's name so long before.[1]

One structural connection casts an ironic hue over all of David's overblown praise for Yahweh. The connection may be schematized, including quotations to show the concrete semantic links that highlight this irony, as follows:

---

1. David's mid-address, ceremonious appellation of Yahweh as "Yhwh Sᵉbaoth, God of Israel," seems a combination of praise and another forged link between the exodus deity and event and the David event.

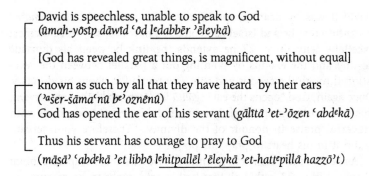

David is speechless, unable to speak to God
(ûmah-yôsîp dāwîd ʿōd lᵉdabbēr ʾēleykā)

[God has revealed great things, is magnificent, without equal]

known as such by all that they have heard by their ears
(ʾᵃšer-šāmaʿnû bᵉʾoznēnû)
God has opened the ear of his servant (gālîtā ʾet-ʾōzen ʿabdᵉkā)

Thus his servant has courage to pray to God
(māṣāʾ ʿabdᵉkā ʾet libbô lᵉhitpallēl ʾēleykā ʾet-hattᵉpillâ hazzōʾt)

Figure 28. Structure in 2 Sam 7.18–29

By the time God hears (and we read) how it was that David took courage in "C'" (v. 27) some seven verses of supposed speechlessness have elapsed.[1] On one hand, the rhetorical gambit in "C" (v. 20) was to feign dumb astonishment at Yahweh's unprecedented generosity. On the other hand, the guise of the entreaty is irrepressible praise. David cannot stop himself, so he pretends, from gushing about all that God has done for Israel and now David. The reader can appreciate David's compulsion to speak, but the narratorial frame exposes a contradiction that taints the rhetoric. The graces of piety demand humble acceptance, but the potential gains are too great to leave to anyone's imagination, most especially God's.[2]

VERSE 27

"C'" (v. 27) is explicitly linked to "C" (vv. 20–22) by its reduplicating reference to auditory revelation. In v. 22 David preened God for the great reputation the god won in the exodus. According to

---

1. The fact of loquacious speech speaks against taking David's fawning rhetoric at face value. Compare some rather more sincere responses to divine speech, e.g. Abram in Gen 12 or Eli in 1 Sam 3.18. What is all this talk from David if not an attempt to remake the divine word (cf. Solomon's long and similar effort in 1 Kgs 8)?

2. Rost (1982:37 [1926]) exemplifies what I would see as a typical careful reader's response to David's aureate rhetoric. "In this way the prayer has something rather vague or colourless about it which stands out strikingly against the single, concrete sentence so powerful in its brevity: 'I will make you a house.' In the face of this all embellishment takes a second place."

David it was by hearing, specifically "with our ears" (*ʾašer šāmaʿnû beʾoznēnû*) that he and Israel had come to know and so extol this most excellent deity. In v. 27 he extends the link between his dynastic destiny and the exodus by pointing out a parallel between the revelation through the exodus and this new revelation about his dynasty. Once again, God "opens the ear" (*gālîtā ʾet ʾōzen ʿabdekā*) of his servant, this time with a promise of dynasty, and his servant responds with prayerful praise in honour of the divinity. "Therefore your servant found it in his heart to pray this prayer to you."

Aside from the connection with "C," David's most emphatic point (2 times) in v. 27 is that all that he has said ought to be received as "prayer": *lehitpallēl ... ʾet-hattepillâ*. The emphasis is in keeping with David's primary guise as someone who seeks only to praise the great god for what he has done. The careful rhetoric aimed at alluring the god into David's trap is ostensibly nothing more than a simple prayer from a humble servant.

VERSE 28

There is little to add to the discussion of the parallels between "Bʹ" (v. 28) and its predecessor, "B" (v. 19). In both verses David adduces the divine origin of the promises, in and of itself, as an argument in favour of irrevocability. God must do as "The God-who-cannot-lie" (*ʾattâ-hûʾ hāʾelōhîm ûdebāreykā yihyû ʾemet*) has said (cf. Num 23.19–20; 1 Sam 15.29).[1] The final twist on David's play with the undefined demonstrative *zōʾt* is to attach it, as an attributive adjective, to "the good" that he claims God has proclaimed to his servant (*ʾet-haṭṭôbâ hazzōʾt*). The characterization of what God has said as "this good," of course, aims at the same thing: to wring all the honey from the divine word while plucking out whatever sting it might contain.

VERSE 29

Within "Aʹ" (v. 29) there is a singular emphasis on enduring blessing, a blessing that affects a "house," the house of "your servant":

---

1. Both Ps. 89 (vv. 1–4, 49) and Ps. 132 (v. 11) rely on the same theological stratagem as David.

ûbārēk	'et-bêt-ʿabdᵉkā	lihyôt lᵉʿôlām lᵉpāneykā
ûmibbirkātᵉkā	bêt-ʿabdᵉkā	lᵉʿôlām

Figure 29. Structure of 2 Sam 7.29

The servant's house, enduring perpetually (*lᵉʿôlām*), is a rhyming transformation of its correspondent in "A" (v. 18), where stood the unworthy house (*ûmî bêtî*) that had been brought "so far" (*ʿad-hᵃlōm*). The same transformation clothes David's new-found confidence in talking about divine activity. In v. 18 he floated a tone of quavering incredulity—"that you should have brought me to this point" (*hᵃbîʾōtanî*, Hiphʿîl perfect). In v. 29 he dismisses all uncertainty with a directive to "bless" (*ûbārēk*, Piʿēl imv.) and caps that with a blessing on his house that takes on life and powers of blessing for itself—"and from your blessing may the house of your servant be blessed" (*yᵉbōrak*, Puʿal jussive).[1] As in v. 28, the imperative "bless" (*ûbārēk*) takes its authority, not from supplicant David, but from the fact that "the Lord Yahweh" has spoken (*kî-ʾattâ … dibbartā*). The supplicant has a perfect shield against any denunciation of trying to lord it over Yahweh.

YAHWEH'S MISSING REBUTTAL

David's speech begs a divine riposte but there is none. One wonders how God could be taken in by such blandishment. Is he as blindly vain, or at least so focused on his goal of world renown, that he cannot see through the guise? The reader never gets to find out, at least not in any immediate or obvious sense, because God does not respond straight-away. Instead, David speech just fades away, unanswered. Any response is displaced by a bland scenic connector: "after this …" and another scene begins. Nothing immediate reveals Yahweh's reading, but it is absolutely clear in all his revelations to Solomon about the perpetuity of the Davidic dynasty. In each case (1 Kgs 3.14; 6.12–13; 9.3–9), continuance utterly depends on obedience and the punishments for disobedience are no less than the covenant curses of the Sinaitic covenant (1 Kgs 9.3–9; Eslinger 1989:144–46; McConville 1992). Yahweh chooses not to disillusion David about his gullibility. To do so would disclose the rhetorical

---

1. The *Puʿal* plays this rhetorical role for David by allowing him to omit any reference to God as subject who would actively bless the house of David.

pitfall that he himself had set and into which David has fallen. Once the bait is taken, however, the temple of David's design has been warded off, and David himself lies cold in the grave, Yahweh dispenses with the ambiguity of the trap and lays all out for Solomon and the reader to see. There can be no doubt that Yahweh saw through the subterfuge as easily as any attentive reader might.

In the face of Yahweh's silence, David can only think that he has succeeded, that Yahweh accepts his revisionism, and that his view of the promises that God has made is correct. And that is exactly the end to which Yahweh's rhetoric has been aimed.

Chapter 4

BIBLICAL ECHOES OF 2 SAMUEL 7

Regarding the question of how we should see the "Davidic" and Sinaitic covenants and their respective positions, the inescapable conclusion is that there is no differentiation and thus no relationship, at least not respecting the rhetoric within 2 Samuel 7. Given that 2 Samuel 7 is the single most important textual foundation of the notion of a Davidic covenant, the concept itself seems poorly based. Jon Levenson quotes John Bright as someone representing the "segregationist" position, one who sees the two "covenants" as radically different and in competition. Bright says, "the covenant with David inevitably tended to crowd the Sinaitic Covenant and its stipulations into the background, thereby setting up a tension between the two" (Levenson 1985:212). But nothing that Yahweh says about perpetuity could crowd his fundamental call to obedience, a call founded on the Sinaitic model. The so-called Sinai covenant, in 2 Samuel 7, is more a presence than a contract—more like a cloud of obligation conjured by Yahweh's heavy-handed recollections of the past. At least, that is how it seems that he expects his recollections to affect his royal auditor. With such a deity as this there can be nothing, ever, that could surmount the basis for relation and obligation that the god establishes with the singular foundational event.

But what about the connection with other biblical passages and with ancient Israelite thought? Is there not a great deal of supporting evidence in the Bible suggesting that some thought about God's treatment of the Davidic house in terms of an everlasting support? One thinks, immediately, of the so-called "Zion theology." But Levenson's recent survey of the evidence for a strong connection between even the house of David and Zion, let alone the eternal election of the house of David and Zion suggests that these are two things and not one.[1] Still, there are

---

1. "It is surely the case that the absence of any language of chosenness in so many of the poems that reflect the Zion traditions casts doubt upon the claim that those traditions were always grounded in election" (J.D. Levenson 1992:1100). In his recent article on Old Testament texts that contribute to the developing notion of a messiah, J.J.M. Roberts offers the following description of "Israelite royal theology" as developed in the kingdom of Judah:

a few passages that do refer, explicitly, to the speeches in 2 Samuel 7 and their interpretations of what was said between God and David require some explanation.

PASSAGES SUPPORTING
AN UNCONDITIONAL DAVIDIC COVENANT

Any argument against a radically new agreement between Yahweh and David in 2 Samuel 7 must address three biblical texts that seem to allude to this chapter, or at least this event. Texts such as Psalm 89 or Psalm 132 or David's recollections in 2 Sam 23.1–7 seem to suppose that God did promise something new (according to Rost (1982:49 [1926]), a historical fact supported by these inner–biblical allusions) and that God could be called to account for it. For present, a-historical purposes there is no need to venture a guess as to which text came first:[1] the concern about relationship has strictly to do with the fact that another biblical text suggests a reading of 2 Samuel 7 contrary to that proposed here. "I've made a covenant with my chosen, I've sworn to David my servant: 'forever I'll establish your seed, and I will maintain, through the generations, your throne'" (Ps 89.4–5). "… for he has installed an eternal covenant for me, in every respect ordered and secure" (David in 2 Sam 23.5).

But do these texts really support a more conventional reading of the "Davidic covenant" in 2 Samuel 7? There is reason to say no. The inner-

> The particular historical developments during the reigns of David and Solomon led to the widely accepted theological claims that Yahweh had chosen David to be his king and Jerusalem to be his royal city. The choice of David extended to David's descendants so that the Davidic dynasty was to retain David's throne in perpetuity and the choice of Jerusalem meant that Yahweh would make his abode there, first in David's tent where David had the ark transferred with great fanfare and then in the Temple that Solomon eventually built" (1992:42).

Roberts' description of the supposed ideology is little more than a paraphrase of the conventional critical reading of 2 Samuel 7. The fact of paraphrase combined with the assumption that there is no need to justify such reliance on such a text, which has such obvious potential for political tendentiousness, shows the degree to which the "Davidic covenant" governs modern study of "royal ideology" and particularly 2 Samuel 7.

1. T.N.D. Mettinger (1976:254 ff.) describes the problems of dating.

biblical reflections, for example, are not unanimous. In its canonical form, Psalm 132 subjects the Davidic dynasty to the condition of obedience: "... if your sons keep my covenant and my testimony which I will teach them ..." (v. 12).[1] And what about David's recollections in 2 Samuel 23? Can these be used as lenses for interpreting the divine rhetoric any more than his counter-rhetoric in ch. 7 itself? Even by 2 Samuel 23, David's view remains an entirely implicated position. He has everything to gain were Yahweh to accept his characterization of the divine statements as an "eternal covenant" (b*erît *ôlām).

Yet, it is useful to try and determine the local rhetorical goals regulating the way these biblical authors read the text of 2 Samuel 7 or the dialogue described therein. Even without detailed rhetorical study the claims of these texts are so strong that all but the most insensitive can scent their rhetorical situation and purpose. Beginning with the most obvious, in 2 Samuel 23 David recapitulates his career and relationship with God. What better time to repeat again his own view of what God had promised him in 2 Samuel 7? David's use of the word "covenant" (v. 12, b*erît*) to characterize what God had granted in 2 Samuel 7 betrays the same grasping quality that typifies his speech in 2 Samuel 7. The absence of that key word in God's speech in 2 Samuel 7 has long troubled those who have followed David's reading of it, even to the point of following David's lead here believing that the 2 Samuel 23 reading is the natural and correct reading of what God says in 2 Samuel 7 (e.g., G. Fohrer 1959:9). But the speech in ch. 23 is David's last bid to put a bright face on the personal disaster[2] (in many ways, a national disaster too, e.g., 2 Sam 19.1–10) that his reign has become. Since the affair with Uriah's wife (2 Sam 11), Nathan's prophecy of ruination to the house of David (2 Sam 12.10–11) has hung over all. The bizarre circumstance surrounding David's census (2 Sam 24, esp. vv. 1, 12–16) show that the words of Israel's self-described "sweet psalmist" (2 Sam

---

1. Cf. Mettinger (1976:256 n. 12), approving of L. Perlitt (1969:52) who sees something other than the Davidic covenant in Psalm 132. That it is the matter of dynastic promise, the same focal point as that of 2 Samuel 7, is not disputed. Mettinger's solution is to make v. 12 a later conditionalization of an allusion to the unconditional covenant in v. 11 (p. 257).

2. Cf. Kruse (1985:148), "... it [2 Sam 23.1–7] is a self-satisfied reflection of the aging monarch ... on the points that had pleased him most." I part from Kruse only in finding wishful thinking, rather than self-satisfied complacency, in David's "last words."

23.1, $ne^{c}tm$ $z^{e}mir\hat{o}t$) do nothing to mollify the deity's anger at the house of David. For present purposes, however, the response of the deity, the most obvious target of David's speech, is less important than David's need to reaffirm that he had won an eternal covenant, God's guarantee of a secure Davidic throne.[1] The present setting of David's last words does more to destabilize the notion of an "eternal covenant" than to entrench it. At the least, it should not be read as retrospective confirmation of some eternal covenant in 2 Samuel 7.[2]

The situation addressed by Psalm 89 is the author's belief that God has breached the covenant ($b^{e}r\hat{\imath}t$, v. 35) that he made with David. Divinity has punished dynasty excessively (vv. 46–48), without good cause, and needs to be reminded of its sealed commitment to the Davidic dynasty.[3] The absence of any reference to a provocation for the divine wrath seems a wise rhetorical choice. The recollection of all God's past acts of benefaction and the stability of the cosmos he created are mentioned in series, just before the detailed reprise[4] of the incident of 2 Samuel 7. In addition to other aims,[5] the series including the Davidic covenant among the acts of creation is designed to emphasize the inherent reliability of what God promised David. It is on the same footing as creation itself and even God ought to honour his fixed

1. Cf. Fokkelman 1990:361), "… the poem's ideological centre of gravity makes clear that the well-being was initiated by God and can proceed through his blessing."

2. To the contrary, L. Rost (1982:49[1926]) accepts the echoes in 2 Samuel 23 and 1 Kgs 2.24 as support for seeing a basis in historical fact for 2 Samuel 7. Rost's credulity, from a more trusting critical age, goes far beyond the acceptance of literary confirmations rejected herein.

3. N.M. Sarna (1963:43–44) goes beyond the implicit indications of rhetorical situation to specify the historical circumstance that might have evoked the psalm.

4. On the disputed question of the relative dating of 2 Samuel 7 and Psalm 89 see Mettinger (1976:255 n. 2) for the lists of recent scholars espousing the two most obvious possibilities. My discussion depends on an agnosticism about historical precedences and places Ps 89 in dependence on 2 Samuel 7 in accord with the arguments (canonical) presented in my article on inner-biblical allusion (Eslinger 1992).

5. "By a skillful transfer of titles from God to David, this psalm places in the king's hands the power of God to bring peace out of chaos, to induce life out of sterility" (C. Stuhlmueller 1988:474; cf. E. Beaucamp 1979:90). Stuhlmueller's reading fits the general tendency of reception: that the overriding purpose of the psalmist is to put God to work on behalf of David and thus Israel.

decrees.[1] The much elaborated description of the covenant (vv. 19–29) and the status it confers on the Davidides also aims to secure the dynasty. The extension of securities offered, going far beyond anything that Yahweh says in 2 Samuel 7, is entirely in keeping with the psalm's overarching rhetorical aims. But the excess should itself caution about using this tendentious psalm as support for an unconditional reading of 2 Samuel 7.[2]

PASSAGES NOT SUPPORTING
AN UNCONDITIONAL DAVIDIC COVENANT

The most problematic passages for an unconditional reading are the series of conditionalized versions of the promises to David, conditionalizations expressed either to (1 Kgs 3.14; 6.12–13; 9.3–9) or by (1 Kgs 8.25) David's immediate successor Solomon. The difference between these passages, which are mostly in the divine voice, and the divine speech in 2 Samuel 7 is obvious and explicit. Consequently, most interpretations have resolved the discrepancy in terms of literary history, specifically source analysis and tradition history.[3] From a synchronic

---

1. Cf. A. Weiser (1962:592), "According to the Old Testament idea of the divine saving rule, Nature and History, Creation and Election, are not to be separated from each other. The eternal reign of God is to be reflected in the sphere of influence of the earthly ruler whom God has adopted as his son (cf. Ps. 2.7 f.). It is for this reason and for this reason only that no limits are to be set to his dominion either in space or time." I agree with Weiser's reading of the rhetorical purpose of the psalm, but differ for reason of not wanting to assign such ideology to the whole of the Bible (Hebrew). Even to say that such was "royal ideology" of the southern kingdom pushes the rhetorical features of the psalm too hard in the direction of direct correspondence with supposed historical entities. Fohrer's political reading (1959:9 n. 17) of the psalmist's attempt to corral God seems closer to the mark.

2. Cf. Sarna (1963:39), "the author of the lament needed to adapt Nathan's oracle to his own immediate purposes. He had not the slightest interest in the original occasion of the oracle .... His sole concern was with the Divine Pledge of perpetuity to the Davidic dynasty as such and with the glaring contrast between the promised ideal and the present reality. It is this exclusive interest that explains the expansion, selectivity, departures from, and changes of emphasis in the psalmist's citations from the text of the oracle."

3. Levenson (1985:211), for example, reads the contradictions in terms of competing ideological conflicts and developments behind the text. "The subordination of the Davidic covenant to the Sinaitic in 1 Kgs 8:25, therefore, must

perspective, the solution is superficially more simple and, theologically, more intricate. Yahweh is free to reveal to Solomon what he concealed from David. The father had to be gulled into accepting the godly version of dynastic security; the son, who has already proven ready to accept a version with strings attached,[1] is preempted with a firm divine hand bearing conditions. Solomon's demonstrated lust for power (1 Kgs 2.12–46; cf. Fokkelman 1981:409; Eslinger 1989:125–29) makes him a ready mark for any suggestion of security on the throne, regardless of conditions. Solomon stands in the place of Israel before, who were only told that the king they had asked was not the king that they had got after it was too late to reject the latter (1 Sam 10.24–27).

But the synchronic view is also more complex because it necessitates explaining why Solomon subsequently reiterates the conditionalized version of the promises. The answer, which can only be obtained by a detailed rhetorical analysis of Solomon's prayer in 1 Kings 8 (see Eslinger 1989:123–81), may be summarized: Solomon accepts, for the most part (Eslinger 1989:160–61), Yahweh's conditions, but parries the thrust by trying to take all the bite out of the covenant curses (compare 1 Kgs 8.31–53 and Deut 28.15–68; Eslinger 1989:163–74). That is to say, Solomon wants to appear to defer to God's claim on his loyalty, but also wants to ensure that the consequences of disobedience are without consequence.

CONCLUSIONS ABOUT THE ECHOES

Each of the inner-biblical reflections on 2 Samuel 7, or more specifically the divine speech in 2 Samuel 7, is made with a view to specific rhetorical goals. In the case of Psalm 89 and Psalm 132 the aim is to underline the inviolability of God's promises, most especially with a view to getting God to honour them. The same holds true for David's

---

be seen as a reinterpretation that reflects the growing canonical status of the Sinaitic traditions that will become the Pentateuch." Fohrer's (1959:10) relative dating—the Solomonic material in 1 Kings antedates the Davidic in 2 Samuel 7—is another simple way to solve the apparent contradiction. The stability of grounds for such an assessment is, however, another matter.

1. He does not balk or even blink when David, in his personal vendetta from the grave, conditionalizes the promises to his own advantage (1 Kgs 2.4).

"last words"[1] in 2 Samuel 23. Tendentious in their own right, these passages hold no promise for an understanding of the rhetoric voiced within 2 Sam 7.

In the case of God's reiterations in 1 Kings the relationship is more complex. First it is the same character voice that underlines the condition of obedience that was not obvious in 2 Samuel 7. Even though we might appreciate the rhetorical strategy with regard to Solomon, it is difficult, especially for a confessional reader, to appreciate how God can take away with one hand what he has granted with the other. Flatly stated, it seems as though God lied to David if what he says to Solomon is his true intent regarding the "Davidic covenant." 'But God is not a man that he should lie ...' (1 Sam 15.29); how can this be? The unconventional solution proposed here (the divide and conquer strategy of source-criticism or tradition history[2] being a well-trodden path out of such theological difficulties) is that God is only making manifest here what was always implicit in his words to David. From a theologically conservative point of view such as my own, it is inviting to take what God says to Solomon in 1 Kings as confirming evidence for such a reading of the divine rhetoric in 2 Samuel 7. From the methodological viewpoint of rhetorical criticism, however, it is inadvisable to do so since the rhetorical situation in 1 Kings has changed. Even though it is the same character discussing the same topic, the local conditions of the discussion, the changing of kings and the weak, insecure position of the incoming monarch, warrant circumspection regarding any equation of what God says to Solomon with what he said to David. In my view, the reading of God's rhetoric in 2 Samuel 7 is strong enough to stand on its own. Proceeding thence to 1 Kings, I have no difficulty recognizing that God is making explicit what was already implicit in his conversation with David. What is determinative of God's statements in 1 Kings is not what he said to David, however: it is, rather, what he

---

1. Of course, as Fokkelman points out, these are not David's final words (1990:355). The speech/poem is recognizable, nevertheless, as David's final wish for a memorial and guarantee of what he thought he had accomplished in his life.

2. E.g., see E. Würthwein (1977:65) on 1 Kgs 6.11–13. B. Halpern (1988:171–74) offers a more extensive discussion of the conditionalizations in 1 Kings. But Halpern is little concerned with solving any supposed theological conundrum and much more with establishing the historical backgrounds that gave rise to the obvious literary difficulty.

wants to impress on Solomon given Solomon's weakness at that moment.

The most prudent course for rhetorical analysis of the divine speech in 2 Samuel 7 is to ignore the inner-biblical allusions to the speech or whatever tradition or event might lie behind it. After each related text has been studied on its own one may explore their relationships. That said, it should be added that the relationship between God's conversations with David and Solomon require related understanding. They are topically related, expressed by the same character, and part of a single causal chain in the same story line. Part of such understanding would involve retrospective assessment, once 1 Kings had been reached, of one's reading of the divine speech in 2 Samuel 7. If one comes to the narrative with any impression at all of the obligatory note that rings through Yahweh's speech in 2 Samuel 7, the resurfacing of that theme at David's death can be absorbed without much difficulty.

2 SAMUEL 7 IN THE CONTEXT OF THE DTR

Dennis McCarthy (1965, "II Samuel 7 and the Structure of the Deuteronomic History") alerted scholars to the important role, both retrospective and prospective, that 2 Samuel 7 plays in the context of the Dtr narrative. But work on "Nathan's Oracle" has mostly overlooked the nuances of voicing and rhetoric in the chapter. This has led to misinterpretation, such as the stock view that the bulk of the chapter is a "key speech" from the prophet Nathan voicing the Dtr's central concerns (e.g., McCarter 1984:217–20). Given a basic regard for the voice structure of this narrative segment and, equally important, given an appreciation of individual character rhetoric, how does the chapter sit in the Dtr narrative? That is to say, what is the representational point of this important conversation between Yahweh and David in the context of the larger narrative?

Paramount in what the chapter reveals is not information about the temple or about the future of the Davidic dynasty. Those are concerns that God knows David is interested in and God addresses them as he works to divert David from his temple project. But those are trivial concerns of a human character within the story world. Such cares are much less interesting than the fascinating insight that we get into the divine character, his concerns, and his plans—past, present and future. From the way that Yahweh evokes the past and transposes it to the present and future one can see how he might turn into the eternal, atemporal God of the theologians. Nothing changes for God: what he has established in the past is brought to bear equally on past, present, and future. Certainly for David the future after 2 Samuel 7 lies in the "Davidic covenant"; but for Yahweh it is obligation (Sinai) as ever. David, along with Israel, is obliged to Yahweh for past benefactions and will remain ever so as Yahweh heaps even more blessings in the bountiful promises of vv. 9–16. But blessing, in Yahweh's economy, brings obligation. Though there may not be any more arbitrary rejections such as Saul's (v. 15), punishment for covenantal disobedience is assured (v. 14).

We see, in this interchange between the calculating king and the god who brooks no rival, the same pattern as was played out in the people's request for a human king. God took that request as an encroachment against divine prerogatives. As soon as opportunity presented itself, God removed the last vestige of imposition and installed his own replacement. Even then the monarchy is deviant, not something integral to the divine plan for the Israelite nation. The parallel instructs because it foreshadows Yahweh's method in 2 Samuel 7. First the request is flatly rejected, but then apparently acceded to, albeit with modification. There will be no house for Yahweh to dwell in, but there will be one for his name and David's seed shall build it. But what is the parallel to the rejection of Saul, since that specific possibility is explicitly excluded by Yahweh in his speech (v. 15)? The obvious place to look is Solomon's temple and Yahweh's attitude toward it. Recalling that David's apparent motivation for wanting the temple was security, we find the same concerns expressed throughout Solomon's statements about the temple he builds (1 Kgs 8.22–61; Eslinger 1989:155–76). Solomon is more forthright about the role that he envisions for the temple in securing his throne. Yahweh's response to such a vision of the temple is a flat rejection, a rejection that comes as close as imaginable to outright contradiction of the tone of the promises to David in 2 Samuel 7 (cf. 1 Kgs 9.4–9 and 2 Sam 7.14–15). The parallel between first allowing Saul and then rejecting him, and first allowing a successor to build a securing temple and then rejecting it, has the characteristic feel of such biblical parallels. Yahweh's strategy, both times, is to enclose the offending action and then smother it. No human initiative can be allowed to interfere with the plan, publicly inaugurated at Sinai, of covenantal interaction between God and Israel. Just as we cannot comprehend why God first rejects a king but then allows one, so scholars have been perplexed about the rejection followed by acceptance of a temple. In both cases the answer only becomes apparent after the opposing party has accepted the modifications that God makes to the original proposition. That done, God's characteristic jealousy over indefeasible divine prerogative surfaces almost immediately (cf. 1 Sam 16.1; 1 Kgs 9.3–9).

What God reveals of himself, to readers but not to David, is a willingness to dissimulate for human characters whose actions intrude on the divine scheme of things. Israel thinks God has granted a king but discovers, too late, that Saul is only a *nāgîd*, a "designate" (cf. Eslinger 1985:303–9, 348–58; 1 Sam 10.24–27). Likewise, David has every reason to believe that he has gotten far more than he bargained for with this temple and enduring dynasty. Too late by far—David is dead—will his son discover that appearance (2 Sam 7) is not reality (1 Kgs 3.14; 6.12–13; 9.4–9).

It is difficult for a reading community with expectations of scrupulous behaviour from divinity to accept such readings. One need belong only to the less committed Western cultural reading community to know that God ought not to do such things. Perhaps a confessional reader must go even further and say that God *cannot* do such things because they are contrary to his nature. Therefore, the reading must be exorcised.

I favour a reverse revision. In the Scripture, God can and does dissimulate in his interaction with humans in the story world (and therefore, by analogy, in his interaction with humans in the real world of the confessing community outside the scriptural text). But the biblical narrative also provides a model for perceiving such action: there is no condemnation for what God does, either in the case of Israel and its king or David and his temple. There is not one word of evaluative language, nor even a single evaluative implication, from the narrator who describes Yahweh as he bends David's will to his inscrutable divine purpose. The narrator's silence begs some explanation. Perhaps the reading is wrong, unthinkable for the monotheistic community who produced this text (so Sternberg 1985:84–128); perhaps there is some subtle condemnation of the divinity's action, though my scrutiny suggests not; perhaps the narrative is a perfect model of objective reportage, refraining from all evaluative commentary so that the dynamic of divine-human interaction can be seen clearly "for what it was"; or perhaps most obvious of all, perhaps it is the narrator's view that what God does is necessary. The end, whatever that may be, justifies the means. Of course one may reject the former and thus condemn the latter, but the narrative seems not to. My own study of the Dtr narrative leads me to see this narrative as conventionally impartial, objective, and in support of whatever unstated course it is that God pursues. One point of all this evaluative silence must be that it is the proper vantage from which to view the failed covenantal dialogue that was ancient Israel's historical existence.[1] Such narratorial neutrality and objectivity, however much a literary convention, constitutes in and of itself a recommended hermeneutic for struggling with the failed experiment. But even more, and especially in such places as divine dissimulation plays a key role in the forward progression of the story, it may be that the narrator sees and wants readers to see the inevitability of God doing what he does. Having entered into a historical relationship with a party that almost never shares his vision, God is forced to modify his design temporarily to accommodate his human partners. He is forced to do what God, in and of itself, would have neither reason nor inclination to do.

So far as the narrative place of the promises that God makes to David, these things are only of secondary importance. Like the allowance of the monarchy before them, the temple and the Davidic dynasty are not allowed to derail the divine scheme for Israel. Their appearance in the address to David is no touchstone, divine or narratorial, for the subsequent course of Israel's existence. They are, rather, topoi in the divine speech to David and have their bearing only within the context of that discourse.

EXCURSUS: A TEMPLE FOR GOD'S NAME/DWELLING

The relation between 2 Samuel 7 and 2 Kgs 25.27–30 has been important in redactional studies of the Dtr narrative. Developing a suggestion by Cross (1973:288), Richard Nelson explains the contradiction between the promises to

---

1. Cf. David Gunn's remarks, "We find in the narrative no simple *Tendenz* or moralizing but rather a picture of the rich variety of life that is often comic and ironic in its contrasting perspectives and conflicting norms. Not that the author is amoral or immoral; but his judgement is tempered by his sense of the intricacy and ambivalence of the situations that confront his characters—a sense, also, that is not without significance for his treatment of Providence in the story" (1978:111). See Eslinger (1989:221–44) for a detailed analysis of evaluative discourse in the Dtr narrative.

David and the ignominious end of the Davidic dynasty as a consequence of a double redaction in which an exilic editor adds the nay-saying material of 2 Kings 25 to bring the narrative into accord with the political reality of his time (1981:89).

> How can a single work offer hope of consistent grace in Judges but no hope of forgiveness for Manasseh's sins, even after Josiah's exemplary repentance? Or how can it encompass unconditional promises for a Davidic dynasty, yet drive the final nail into the coffin of that dynasty with 2 Kings 25:27–30? All attempts to harmonize these tensions have proven unsatisfactory because they never took into account the dual nature of the present form of the Deuteronomistic history as the work of two theologians working in two quite different periods of history (1981:120).

The reading offered here, as does Nelson's, sides with those who find a less than bright prospect for the house of David in 2 Kgs 25.27–30 (cf. Cross's comments on positive readings of the passage, 1973:277; Nelson 1981:149 n. 8). But I find no contradiction between what Yahweh says in 2 Samuel 7 and what happens at the conclusion 2 Kings 25. On the basis of these two important passages alone, therefore, my reading has no need of doubled redaction.

No doubt supporters of the redactional division for the Dtr will point to the famous *nîr* passages intervening between 2 Samuel 7 and 2 Kgs 25.27–30 (1 Kgs 11.36; 15.4; 2 Kgs 8.19, on which, see Nelson's thorough review, 1981:108–18). Had Yahweh not promised David something very much like an eternal dynasty, why would both Yahweh (1 Kgs 11.36) and the narrator (1 Kgs 15.4; 2 Kgs 8.19) adduce the "Davidic covenant" as a reason for the continuation of the Davidic house when there was sufficient warrant for its end? The problem thus raised seems insuperable until one looks more closely at what is said about this leniency on behalf of David. In 1 Kings 11 Yahweh is imposing a punishment, hardly a mild one, and he does it for want of obedience (1 Kgs 11.33). But the punishment is ameliorated for the sake of David, noteworthy for having been chosen and for his own obedience (v. 34). The sequence of reference is important. Yahweh honours first his own action and secondarily his designate's dutious behaviour. Clemency here is residual, not systemic. Whether one reads *nîr* as "royal prerogative" (cf. Nelson 1981:109, citing Wevers and Hanson) or as "lamp," what is allowed is specifically tied to David's behaviour as "my servant"—not to the promise of a "house." Before we look at what the narrator adds to this motif, it is also worth noting that God uses different temporal terminology to describe the duration of this clemency. From "for ever" (*'ad-'ôlām*) in 2 Samuel 7 (cf. especially v. 16) Yahweh shifts to "all the days before him" (*kol-hayyāmîm*) in 1 Kgs 11.36. There is no large difference in temporal terms of reference: both terms refer to an extended, but not eternal, duration. But the first, used on David, has the grander ring, while the second—"for David, my servant, all the days before him"—is intentionally diminished by its strong association with the dead king. What we have here is a contextually implicated use of words, not a dictionary entry.

Of course Yahweh does allude to the promises to David in this monologue, but it is with the same conditionalizing emphasis that he used to relate the promises to Solomon (1 Kgs 11.38; cf. 3.14; 6.12–13; 9.4–9). Obedience is critical. There is irony too: it is in the same breath with which he strips the Davidides of power that Yahweh promises Jeroboam a "faithful house" (*bayit-ne'eman*) like that built for David (cf. 2 Sam 7.16). Either God is disingenuous or his own views about the "Davidic covenant" are other than what modern commentators understand about it.

In 1 Kgs 15.4 the narrator explains the unexpected survival of a Davidide, Abiyam, on the throne. The simple fact that an explanation is provided for the continuation of a sinner suggests that the narrator finds it unusual in the light of what has gone before. Again, the reason for the unusual state of affairs is not any eternal covenant; it is the residual effect of David's own fidelity to the commands of Yahweh. Continuance comes from someone's obedience and David's stock, the play with Bathsheba not withstanding, is enough to perdure—at least for a while. A subsidiary point, developed from Yahweh's own "lamp" saying in 1 Kgs 11.36, is the shifting emphasis toward Jerusalem and the necessity of its maintenance. Yahweh had specifically mention Jerusalem, "the city in which I have chosen to put my name" (cf. 2 Sam 7.13) as the place where David's "lamp" would be maintained. Already here we see the stake that Yahweh's name has in Jerusalem's survival. The narrator repeats God's emphasis on Jerusalem (*birušalaim*) and underlines it by adding that Yahweh's purpose is to "establish Jerusalem" (*ulehaʿamid 'et-yerušalaim*).

In 2 Kgs 8.19 the narrator again explains the unexpected survival of the nation in the reign of the sinner, Jehoram. Again, it is on account of David, God's servant (*lemaʿan dawid 'abdô*) to whom a "lamp" (*nîr*) had been promised "all the days." Of course no such item had been promised to David exactly; perhaps the narrator refers to 1 Kgs 11.36 as a posthumous award. If we are generous and grant such liberal reference the emphasis on obedience as the condition of a *nîr* remains: it is for David the servant, not David the promisee, that the *nîr* is preserved. If we are not so tolerant of the change in the topic matter spoken to David, then we can take it as the narrator's redescription, in his own words, of what God had offered David. In such case, given that Yahweh defines the operative meaning and context of *nîr* in this issue, it is clear that the narrator means to shrink the grandiloquent offering of 2 Sam 7.

The course of events in the subsequent narrative confirms this reduced assessment of the importance of dynasty and temple in the narrative. Whatever security the temple seemed to contain is denied absolutely by God in 1 Kings (6.12–13; 9.3–9). As for the Davidic dynasty, it is gutted already in the next generation and withers to a shadow by the end of 2 Kings. The parallel description of Mephibosheth, scion of the house of Saul, and Jehoiachin, of the house of David, sitting at the tables of the kings who subdued their dynasty (cf. 2 Sam 9.7, 10, 13: *weʾattā tōʾkal leḥem ʿal-šulḥānī tāmīd*; 2 Kgs 25.29: *weʾākal leḥem tāmīd lepānāyw*) shows how little impact the "Davidic covenant" made. As it was with the house of Saul, so it is with the house of David.[1] Of course it is not exactly the same, for the demise of the house of David comes by way of the Babylonian king instead of the direct affliction by the hand of God—the rod of men versus the terrorism of God (cf. 1 Sam 16.14; *bʿt*). The parallel is only drawn, not commented on, by the narrator. Unlike the modern critical commentator who finds here an unbroachable contradiction, the narrator leaves the stark negation of the promises without expositional adornment. Moreover, the parallel with Mephibosheth seems an intentional augmentation. The point, of course, is not to make the hollowness of the promises in 2 Samuel 7 echo, though I take the echo as confirmation. Rather, the emptiness of what is granted to David echoes an assisting hollow boum[2] to magnify the whimper with which the house of David expires.

1. Cf. J.J. Granowski (1992:183–84), who thanks Peter Miscall (1986:22) for alerting him to the connection. Granowski offers more detailed comparison of similarities and differences between the two passages, along with a reading of the connection's implication contrary to that proposed here.

2. "Hope, politeness, the blowing of a nose, the squeak of a boot, all produce 'boum,' E.M. Forster, *A Passage to India* (1924; Penguin 1936, p. 145).

Bibliography

Ahlström, G.W.
   1961   "Der Prophet Nathan und der Tempelbau," *VT* 11, 113–127.
Anderson, A.A.
   1989   *2 Samuel* (Word Biblical Commentary 11; Dallas, TX: Word Books).
Beaucamp, E.
   1979   *Le Psautier. Vol. II. Ps 73–150* (Paris: J. Gabalda).
Berlin, A.
   1990   "Review, L. Eslinger, *Into the Hands of the Living God*" (Sheffield: Almond, 1989)," *Bib* 71, 561–64.
Betz, H.D.
   1979   *Galatians* (Hermeneia; Philadelphia: Fortress Press).
Botterweck, G.J.
   1986   "yada'," *TDOT* 6 (ed. G.J. Botterweck and H. Ringgren; Grand Rapids, MI: Wm. B. Eerdmans), 468–70.
Bright, J.
   1976   *Covenant and Promise* (Philadelphia: Westminster Press).
Brueggemann, W.
   1990   *First and Second Samuel* (Louisville, KY: John Knox Press).
Busink, T.A.
   1970   *Der Tempel von Jerusalem von Salomo bis Herodes; eine archäologisch-historische Studie unter Berücksichtigung des westsemitischen Tempelbaus. I. Der Tempel Salamos* (Nederlands Instituut voor het Nabije Oosten, Studia Francisci Scholten Memoriae Dicata 3; Leiden: E.J. Brill).
Campbell, A.F.
   1986   *Of Prophets & Kings. A Late Ninth-Century Document (1 Samuel 1 – 2 Kings 10)* (CBQ Monograph Series 17; Washington, DC: Catholic Biblical Assoc. of America).
Campbell, A.F.
   1989/92   *The Study Companion to Old Testament Literature: An Approach to the Writings of Pre-Exilic and Exilic Israel.* (Collegeville, MN: Liturgical Press).
Campbell, A.F., and O'Brien, M.A.
   1993   *Sources of the Pentateuch. Texts, Introductions, Annotations* (Minneapolis, MN: Fortress Press).

Corbett, E.P.J.
1990 *Classical Rhetoric for the Modern Student* (3rd edn; Oxford: Oxford University Press).

Coste, D.
1989 *Narrative as Communication* (Theory and History of Literature 64; Minneapolis, MN: University of Minnesota Press).

Cross, F.M.
1973 *Canaanite Myth and Hebrew Epic. Essays in the History of the Religion of Israel* (Cambridge: Harvard University Press).

Crystal, D.
1987 *The Cambridge Encyclopedia of Language* (Cambridge: Cambridge University Press).

De Vries, S.J.
1985 *1 Kings* (Vol. 12; Word Biblical Commentary; Waco, TX: Word Books).

de Wette, W.M.L.
1858 *A Critical and Historical Introduction to the Canonical Scriptures of the Old Testament* (Vol. 1; trans. Theodore Parker; 2rd edn; Boston: Little, Brown and Co.).

Dhorme, E.P.
1910 *Les Livres de Samuel* (Études Bibliques; Paris: Gabalda).

Driver, S.R.
1913 *Notes on the Hebrew Text of the Books of Samuel with an Introduction on Hebrew Palaeography and the Ancient Versions and Facsimiles of Inscriptions* (2nd edn; Oxford: Clarendon Press).

Dumbrell, W.J.
1988 "The Prospect of Unconditionality in the Sinai Covenant," *Israel's Apostasy and Restoration* (ed. A. Gileadi; Grand Rapids, MI: Baker Book House), 141–55.

Engnell, I.
1949 *The Call of Isaiah. An Exegetical and Comparative Study* (Uppsala Universitets Årsskrift 4; Uppsala / Leipzig: A.-B. Lundequistska bokhandeln / O. Harrassowitz).

Eslinger, L.
1985 *Kingship of God in Crisis. A Close Reading of 1 Samuel 1–12* (BLS 10; Sheffield & Decatur, GA: Almond Press).
1989 *Into the Hands of the Living God* (BLS 24; Sheffield: Sheffield Academic Press).
1991 "Freedom or Knowledge? Perspective & Purpose in the Exodus Narrative (Exodus 1–15)," *JSOT* 52, 43–60.

1992 "Inner-biblical Exegesis and Inner-biblical Allusion: The Question of Category," *VT* 42, 47–58.

Fish, S.E.
1967 *Surprised by Sin: the Reader in Paradise Lost* (Berkeley, Los Angeles & London: University of California Press).

Fohrer, G.
1959 "Der Vertrag zwischen König und Volk in Israel," *ZAW* 71, 1–22.

Fokkelman, J.P.
1981 *Narrative Art and Poetry in the Books of Samuel. King David (II Sam. 9–20 & I Kings 1–2)* (Vol. 1; Assen: Van Gorcum).
1990 *Narrative Art and Poetry in the Books of Samuel. Throne and City (II Sam. 2–8 & 21–24)* (Vol. 3; trans. Mrs. L.Waaning-Wardle; Assen/Mastricht: Van Gorcum).

Fowler, A.
1982 *Kinds of Literature. An Introduction to the Theory of Genres and Modes* (Cambridge, MA: Harvard University Press).

Frankfort, H.
1948 *Kingship and the Gods. A Study of Ancient Near Eastern Religion as the Integration of Society & Nature* (Phoenix Edition, 1978; Chicago & London: University of Chicago Press).

Freedman, R.E.
1987 "The Hiding of the Face: An Essay on the Literary Unity of Biblical Narrative," *Judaic Perspectives on Ancient Israel* (ed. B.E. Levine and E.S. Frerichs; Philadelphia: Fortress Press), 207–22.

Freyne, S.
1988 *Galilee, Jesus and the Gospels. Literary Approaches and Historical Investigations* (Philadelphia: Fortress Press).

Frye, N.
1970 *The Stubborn Structure: Essays on Criticism and Society* (Ithaca, NY: Cornell University Press).

Geiger, A.
1928 *Urschrift und Übersetzungen der Bibel in ihrer Abhängigkeit von der innern Entwicklung des Judenthums* (2nd edn [1857 orig.]; Breslau: Hainauer).

Gileadi, A.
1988 "The Davidic Covenant: A Theological Basis for Corporate Protection," *Israel's Apostasy and Restoration* (ed. A. Gileadi; Grand Rapids, MI: Baker Book House), 157–63.

Granowski, J.J.
1992 "Jehoiachin at the King's Table: A Reading of the Ending of the Second Book of Kings," *Reading Between the Texts. Intertextuality and the Hebrew Bible* (ed. D.N. Fewell; Literary Currents in Biblical Interpretation; Louisville, KY; Westminster/John Knox Press), 153–71.

Greenfield, J.
1985 "Ba'als Throne and Isa 6:1," *Mélanges bibliques et orientaux en l'honneur de M. Mathias Delcor* (ed. A. Caquot, S. Légasse and M. Tardieu; AOAT; Neukirchen-Vluyn: Neukirchener Verlag), 193–98.

Greenstein, E.L.
1988 "On the Genesis of Biblical Prose Narrative," *Prooftexts* 8, 347–63.

Gunn, D.M.
1978 *The Story of King David. Genre and Interpretation* (JSOTSup 6; Sheffield: JSOT).

Gunneweg, A.H.J.
1960 "Sinai Bund und Davidsbund," *VT* 10, 335–41.

Halpern, B.
1981 *The Constitution of the Monarchy in Israel* (HSM 25; Chico, CA: Scholars Press).
1988 *The First Historians. The Hebrew Bible and History* (San Francisco: Harper & Row).

Hauge, M.R.
1975 "The Struggles Of The Blessed In Estrangement II," *ST* 29, 113–46.

Herrnstein Smith, B.
1988 *Contingencies of Value: Alternative Perspectives for Critical Theory* (Cambridge, MA: Harvard University Press).

Hurowitz, V.
1992 *I Have Built You an Exalted House. Temple Building in the Bible in Light of Mesopotamian and Northwest Semitic Writings* (JSOTSup 115; Sheffield: Sheffield Academic Press).

Ishida, T.
1977 *The Royal Dynasties in Ancient Israel* (BZAW 142; Berlin: A. Töpelmann).

Keel, O.
1977 *Jahwe-Visionen und Siegelkunst. Eine neue Deutung der Majestätsschilderungen in Jes 6, Ez 1 und 10 und Sach 4* (Stuttgarter Bibelstudien 84/85; Stuttgart: Verlag Katholisches Bibelwerk).

Keil, C.F., and Delitzsch, F.
1982 *The Books of Samuel* (repr. of 1880 translation published b y T. & T. Clark [Edinburgh]; trans. J. Martin; Grand Rapids, MI: Wm. B. Eerdmans).

Kennedy, G.A.
1984 *New Testament Interpretation through Rhetorical Criticism* (Studies in Religion; Chapel Hill, N.C.; University of North Carolina Press).

Kessler, M.
1974 "A Methodological Setting for Rhetorical Criticism," *Semitics* 4, 22–36.
1980 "An Introduction To Rhetorical Criticism of the Bible: Prolegomena," *Semitics* 7, 1–27.

Kikawada, I.M.
1977 "Some Proposals for the Definition of Rhetorical Criticism," *Semitics* 5, 67–91.

Kruse, H.
1985 "David's Covenant," *VT* 35, 139–64.

Kuenen, A.
1894 *Kritische Methode* (Gesammelte Abhandlungen zur biblischen Wissenschaft; Freiburg: J.C..B. Mohr).

Kumaki, F.K.
1981 "The Deuteronomistic Theology of the Temple—as crystallized in 2 Sam 7, 1 Kgs 8," *AJBI* 7, 16–52.

Leech, G.N.
1969 *A Linguistic Guide to English Poetry* (Essex: Longman).

Levenson, J.D.
1979 "The Davidic Covenant and Its Modern Interpreters," *CBQ* 41, 205–19.
1985 *Sinai and Zion. An Entry into the Jewish Bible* (New York: Winston Press).
1992 "Zion Traditions," *The Anchor Bible Dictionary* (ed. D.N. Freedman, *et al.*; New York: Doubleday), 1098–1102.

Levine, B.A.
1987 "Biblical Temple," *The Encyclopedia of Religion* (ed. M. Eliade, *et al.*; New York: Macmillan Co.), 202–17.

Levinson, Bernard M.
   1991   "The Right Chorale: From the Poetics to the Hermeneutics of the Hebrew Bible," *"Not in Heaven." Coherence and Complexity in Biblical Narrative* (ed. J.P. Rosenblatt and J.C.J. Sitterson; Bloomington & Indianapolis: Indiana University Press), 129–53.

Love, M.
   1990   *The Restrictions of Yahweh's Promises to David in 2 Samuel 7* (B.A. Honours thesis; Calgary: University of Calgary).

Mack, B.L.
   1990   *Rhetoric and the New Testament* (Guides to Biblical Scholarship, New Testament Series; Minneapolis: Fortress).

McCarter, P.K.
   1984   *II Samuel* (AB 9; Garden City, NY: Doubleday & Co.).

McCarthy, D.J.
   1965   "II Samuel 7 and the Structure of the Deuteronomic History," *JBL* 84, 131–8.

McConville, J.G.
   1992   "1 Kings VIII 46–53 and the Deuteronomic Hope," *VT* 42, 67–79.

Mettinger, T.N.D.
   1976   *King and Messiah. The Civil and Sacral Legitimation of the Israelite Kings* (ConBOT 8; Lund: C.W.K. Gleerup).

Meyers, C.
   1987   "David as Temple Builder," *Ancient Israelite Religion. Essays in Honor of Frank Moore Cross* (ed. P.D.J. Miller, P.D. Hanson and S.D. McBride; Philadelphia: Fortress Press), 357–76.

Miscall, P.D.
   1986   *1 Samuel: A Literary Reading* (Indiana Studies in Biblical Literature; Bloomington: Indiana University Press).

Moulton, R.G.
   1908   *The Literary Study of the Bible* (rev. edn of 1895; Boston: D.C. Heath & Co.).

Muilenburg, J.
   1969   "Form Criticism And Beyond," *JBL* 88, 1–17.

Nelson, R.D.
   1981   *The Double Redaction of the Deuteronomistic History* (JSOTSup 18; Sheffield: JSOT).

Nohrnberg, J.C.
  1991 "Princely Characters," *"Not in Heaven." Coherence and Complexity in Biblical Narrative* (ed. J.P. Rosenblatt and J.C.J. Sitterson; Bloomington & Indianapolis: Indiana University Press), 58–97.

Noth, M.
  1957 "David und Israel in II Samuel, 7," *Mélanges Bibliques rédigés en l'Honneur de André Robert* (Travaux de l'Institut Catholique de Paris 4; Paris: Bloud & Gay), 122–30.

  1972 *A History of Pentateuchal Traditions* (trans. Bernard W. Anderson; Englewood Cliffs, NJ: Prentice-Hall).

Ota, M.
  1974 "A Note on 2 Sam 7," *A Light unto My Path. Old Testament Studies in Honor of Jacob M. Myers* (ed. H.N. Bream, R.D. Heim and C.A. Moore; Philadelphia: Temple University Press), 403–7.

Patrick, D., and Scult, A.
  1990 *Rhetoric and Biblical Interpretation* (Sheffield: Almond Press).

Perelman, C. and Olbrechts-Tyteca, L.
  1969 *The New Rhetoric. A Treatise on Argumentation* (trs. John Wilkinson, Purcell Weaver; Notre Dame: University of Notre Dame Press).

Perelman, C.
  1982 *The Realm of Rhetoric* (trans. W. Kluback; Notre Dame: University of Notre Dame Press).

Perlitt, L.
  1969 *Bundestheologie im Alten Testament* (WMANT 36; Neukirchen-Vluyn: Neukirchener Verlag).

Roberts, J.J.M.
  1992 "The Old Testament's Contribution to Messianic Expectations," *The Messiah. Developments in Earliest Judaism and Christianity* (ed. J.H. Charlesworth; Minneapolis: Fortress Press), 39–51.

Rost, L.
  1982 *The Succession to the Throne of David* (Historic Texts and Interpreters in Biblical Scholarship 1; trans. M.D. Rutter, D.M. Gunn; Sheffield: Almond Press).

Saadya Gaon
  1956 *The Book of Doctrines and Beliefs* (trans. Alexander Altmann; Oxford: Oxford University Press).

Sarna, N.M.
1963 "Psalm 89: A Study In Inner Biblical Exegesis," *Biblical And Other Studies* (ed. A. Altmann; Cambridge: Harvard), 29–46.

Schwartz, R.M.
1991 "The Histories of David: Biblical Scholarship and Biblical Stories," *"Not in Heaven." Coherence and Complexity in Biblical Narrative* (ed. J.P. Rosenblatt and J.C.J. Sitterson; Bloomington & Indianapolis: Indiana University Press), 192–210.

Smith, H.P.
1899 *A Critical and Exegetical Commentary on the Books of Samuel* (Edinburgh: T. & T. Clark).

Sternberg, M.
1985 *The Poetics of Biblical Narrative. Ideological Literature and the Drama of Reading* (Bloomington, IN: Indiana University Press).

Stuhlmueller, C.
1988 "Psalms," *Harper's Bible Commentary* (ed. J.L.Mays *et al.*; San Francisco: Harper & Row), 433–94.

Tsevat, M.
1964 "Studies in the Book of Samuel. III The Steadfast House: What was David Promised in II Sam. 7:11b–16," *HUCA* 34, 71–82.
1980 "The Steadfast House. What Was David Promised in 2 Samuel 7?," *The Meaning of the Book of Job and Other Biblical Studies* (New York: KTAV), 101–17.

Unterman, J.
1985 "Covenant," *Harper's Bible Dictionary* (ed. P.J.Achtemeier *et al.*; San Francisco: Harper & Row), 190–92.

Vannoy, J.R.
1978 *Covenant Renewal at Gilgal. A Study of 1 Samuel 11.14–12.25* (Cherry Hill: Mack Pub. Co.).

Veijola, T.
1975 *Die ewige Dynastie. David und die Entstehung seiner Dynastie nach der deuteronomistischen Darstellung* (Annales Academiae Scientiarum Fennicae B193; Helsinki: Suomalainen Tiedeakatemia).
1977 *Das Königtum in der Beurteilung der deuteronomistischen Historiographie* (Helsinki: Suomalainen Tiedeakatemia).

von Nordheim, E.
1977 "König und Tempel. Der Hintergrund der Tempel-bauverbotes in 2 Samuel vii," *VT* 27, 434–53.

von Rad, G.
1962 *Old Testament Theology. The Theology of Israel's Historical Traditions* (Vol. 1; trans. D.M.G. Stalker; New York: Harper & Row).

Waetjen, H.C.
1989 *A Reordering of Power. A Sociopolitical Reading of Mark's Gospel* (Minneapolis: Fortress Press).

Waltke, B., and O'Connor, M.
1990 *An Introduction to Biblical Hebrew Syntax* (Winona Lk, IN: Eisenbrauns).

Waltke, B.K.
1988 "The Phenomenon of Conditionality within Unconditional Covenants," *Israel's Apostasy and Restoration* (ed. A. Gileadi; Grand Rapids, MI: Baker Book House), 124–39.

Watson, W.G.E.
1984 *Classical Hebrew Poetry. A Guide to its Techniques* (JSOTSup 26; Sheffield: JSOT Press).

Weinfeld, M.
1970 "The Covenant of Grant in the Old Testament and in the Ancient Near East," *JAOS* 90, 184–203.

Weiser, A.
1962 *The Psalms* (OTL; Philadelphia: Westminster Press).
1965 "Die Tempelbaukrise unter David," *ZAW* 77, 153–68.

Wellhausen, J.
1871 *Der Text der Bücher Samuelis untersucht* (Göttingen: Vandenhoeck & Ruprecht).
1899 *Die Composition des Hexateuchs und der historischen Bücher des Alten Testaments* (3rd edn; Berlin: Reimer).

Widengren, G.
1952 *Sakrales Königtum im alten Testament und im Judentum* (Stuttgart: W. Kohlhammer).

Wuellner, W.
1987 "Where is Rhetorical Criticism Taking Us?," *CBQ* 49, 448–63.

Würthwein, E.
1977 *Die Bücher der Könige. 1. Könige 1–16* (Göttingen: Vandenhoeck & Ruprecht).

INDEX OF AUTHORS

Olbrechts-Tyteca, L. 29, 30
Ota, M. 16, 43
Patrick, D. 4
Perelman, Ch. 23, 29, 30, 66, 74
Perlitt, L. 91
Roberts, J.J.M. 89–90
Rost, L. 25, 26, 41, 45, 85, 90, 92
Saadya Gaon 72
Sarna, N.M. 92, 93
Schwartz, R. 57
Scult, P. 4
Smith, H.P. 70, 75
Sternberg, M. 98
Stuhlmueller, C. 92
Thenius, O. 31
Tsevat, M. 3, 11, 46, 62

Unterman, J. 2
Vannoy, J.R. 83
Veijola, T. 25, 45, 75, 82
von Nordheim, E. 15
von Rad, G. 11
Waetjen, H. 52
Waltke, B. 1, 25, 31, 79
Watson, W.G.E. 65
Weinfeld, M. 62
Weiser, A. 57, 93
Wellhausen, J. 31, 77, 78
Whybray, R.N. 26
Widengren, G. 23
Wuellner, W. 5, 9, 13
Würthwein, E. 95

INDEX OF HEBREW WORDS

INDEX OF SUBJECTS

INDEX OF BIBLICAL CITATIONS

2 Sam 24	91	1 Kgs 8.27	34
1 Kgs 1.13	75	1 Kgs 8.31–53	94
1 Kgs 1.17	75	1 Kgs 9.3–9	93, 98
1 Kgs 1.20	75	1 Kgs 9.3	47
1 Kgs 1.24	75	1 Kgs 11.21	44
1 Kgs 1.27	75	1 Kgs 11.33	100
1 Kgs 1.30	75	1 Kgs 11.36	101
1 Kgs 1.35	75	1 Kgs 15.4	101
1 Kgs 1.48	75	1 Kgs 16.11	75
1 Kgs 2.12	75	1 Kgs 22.10	75
1 Kgs 2.12–46	94	2 Kgs 8.19	101
1 Kgs 2.19	75	2 Kgs 10.30	75
1 Kgs 2.33	48	2 Kgs 11.19	75
1 Kgs 3.6	75	2 Kgs 13.13	75
1 Kgs 3.12–13	62	2 Kgs 15.12	75
1 Kgs 3.14	93, 98	2 Kgs 25.27–30	3–4, 99–100
1 Kgs 6–7	16	2 Kgs 25.29	101–102
1 Kgs 6.12–13	93, 98	Isa 6.1	75
1 Kgs 8	85, 94	Ps 89	86, 90, 92–93, 94–95
1 Kgs 8.13	34		
1 Kgs 8.17	34	Ps 132	86, 90, 91, 94–95
1 Kgs 8.20	75		
1 Kgs 8.25	75, 93		

JOURNAL FOR THE STUDY OF THE OLD TESTAMENT

Supplement Series